RUNNING FREE

PUBLICATIONS BY THE SAME AUTHOR:

Afrikaans Books:

Die Hel se SpeelgrOnde (1950)
Liefde vir Celia (1951)

English Books:

How To Meditate (Radial Press, Chicago, 1971-72)
How To Find Yourself (Radial Press, Chicago, 1972)

Music Albums:

Africa Belongs to the Lion (Capitol Records, Hollywood)
Moses in Story and Song, (Larrabee Records, L.A.)
Sing! People of God, Sing! (Franciscan Communications, L.A.)
Happy the Man (Franciscan Communications, L.A.)
Good Good (Franciscan Communications, L.A.)
Genesis Too (Franciscan Communications, L.A.)
Keep Your Eyes on Me (Franciscan Communications, L.A.)
God is a Fire of Love (GIA Records, Chicago)
And the Waters Keep on Running through my Mind (GIA)
The Universe is Singing (GIA Records, Chicago)
Great Day in Bethlehem (GIA Records, Chicago)
Voice in the Wilderness (Mayhew-McCrimmon, England)

Running Free

Poems by

Sebastian Temple

WENZEL PRESS

The poem "*I Walk a Razor's Edge,*" published as a frontispiece in the author's book "*How To Meditate,*" copyright 1971-72, is used by permission from Radial Press.

Library of Congress Cataloging-in-Publication Data

Temple, Sebastian, 1928–
    Running free : poems / by Sebastian Temple.
       p.   cm.
    Includes index.
    ISBN 0-930887-26-3 : $19.95
    1. Christian poetry, American. I. Title.
PS3570.E54R86 1995
811' .54--dc20   94-31971
                                                  CIP

Copyright © 1995 by Sebastian Temple. All rights reserved.

Write for a free catalog to:

WENZEL PRESS
P. O. Box 14789-B
Long Beach, CA 90803

DEDICATED TO:

Marno McCarley

Preface

Thou art the singer

Thou art the singer
sing through me.
Thou art the song
sung by thee.
Thou art the listeners
hearing thee.
O sing and be sung
and be sung to through me.

It is not usual for poets to write a foreword to their works. They let the poems speak for themselves. But since many people know me as *"Happy the Man,"** they might wonder if the singer-evangelist that they know was just a polished Hollywood fake, like the city he used to live in.

The dark, painful experiences of some of the poems need to be explained otherwise it would be in distinct conflict with the pictures these good folks may have of me in their minds.

Some years ago I was re-reading *"The Ascent of Mount Carmel"* by St. John of the Cross. I was highly stimulated by it and prayed that God would begin the purification of the passive dark night within me.

Little did I know what I was asking for! At first my meditations were so glorious that I thought I had already reached the pinnacle of Mount Carmel, where only the Honor and Glory of God remains. But it was sheer self-delusion and in hindsight that proved more than anything how badly I was in need of this purification.

After daily being "in heaven," slowly the consolations began to withdraw and I drifted into the dark night—for me a terrible depression that ravaged me so completely that at times I thought that I would die, or worse, that I wouldn't die—or just go completely insane.

Psychologists call this a clinical depression, and it had all the symptoms, but I saw priests who knew the signs and symptons of this state. They said it was the dark night.

But I couldn't believe either group for I was totally controlled by inner doubts, confusion, and negative thoughts.

Finally I got out of it years later. I "finally got out of it" at least four times! The last one was so agonizing that I thought I had already lost my reason... It lasted a whole year and was my season in hell.

· Not that every day was the same. It wasn't. Suddenly in the darkest night the sun would rise and I was convinced that it was over and that I was free. Everything seemed to indicate that I was free. But it wasn't so.

It seemed a very cruel and sadistic way, but now I realize that each "glorious state" was an experience of "Divine Union," and a prelude to a newer and darker state in which all meaning, relevance and energy was completely withdrawn.

This is why this volume is punctuated by these poems in which I tried to analyze the dark night and to give me a space to escape into.

Sebastian Temple

*An album of songs in the spirit of St. Francis of Assisi.

My friend Poetry

Poetry is my ablest friend,
disclosing how I am inside,
on whom I always can depend
to tell me all and to confide
what I do not care to know
or hidden faults I will not show.

It reveals my shadow self to me,
also the lies to which I bow,
presenting unrelentingly
the truth I often disavow
and calling me to face the charges
that my own denial enlarges.

It is your silent voice in me,
showing what I must correct,
pointing out dispassionately
what areas I should dissect
until I know its source and cure
and what to handle or endure.

I thank you for this written voice,
and ongoing revelation
that always presents me the choice
of how to end my isolation,
for as you write these words through me
they forge my inner destiny.

The world I see

The world I see out there
is born from me.
The womb from which it sprung
my fertile mind.
The loins that lit its flame
so I can find
it in the dark of life is me!
The spark I give
the joy that makes it live.

I am its yesterday, today and tomorrow.
I am its gradient of pain and sorrow.
I give each mood and attitude that exude
and permeates its frame,
its changefulness and rangefulness
that constitute the game.

In its wideness I also dwell,
shaping here my heaven and hell,
blaming me, not God or fate
from where my trials originate.

Love and lust

Love is a silence
but lust is a roar.

Love is satisfied
but lust needs more.

Love is a giving
while lust only takes.

Love is a mending
of hearts that lust breaks.

I walk a razor's edge

I walk a razor's edge where few men go
to seek a knowledge that so few men know
and as I climb each high and craggy peak
to learn a language that so few men speak
I glimpse the universe beyond the mind
which goal and destiny I am to find.

There is no one here to show the way,
to guide the path I walk from day to day.
I walk in darkness of a faith and prayer,
a tightrope dangling over sheer despair.
It's here I trace its source and I begin
to see all starts and ends in my within.

Although I have no wings I soar in thought.
I see that what I sell is what I bought.
It's when I meditate that I can find
the universe that's locked beyond my mind.
In quietness I sense the god that's me!
the resurrected one, unborn and free.

Just one false step and down, deep down I fall.
I have to give myself, my very all.
And as I balance between the heart and mind
to break desires that restrict and bind
I find to my surprise I have to be
the very thing I fear before I can be free.

I walk a razor's edge where few men dare.
It leads to the within which few can bear.
It's like the moon that shows one side
to earth and earthly things, only to hide
the universe that blooms deep within my soul,
the fire that I am, the bursting whole!

The divine conquest

So gently did you conquer me
that it took me years to see
that the man I used to be
was vanquished in your victory!
That my dreams were all erased
by the very one they faced.

In loving you my mind got purified
and took on your form and fire.
By obeying yours my own will died
in the cremation of its desire.
Through my prayers you took possession
'till you became my sole obsession.

Yet all the time I still believed
I was in charge, but now I see
how delightfully I was deceived
since you have been replacing me!
To capture both my love and reason
you conquered me with holy treason.

For in my loving and obeying,
in my self-control and praying
I lost myself so much in you
that whom I was is truly dead
and what I loved to pursue
I have now become instead.

That's how you defeated me!
by showing yourself as the I,
that so amazed and deleted me
that what I was could only die
or stand aside to see how you
are living through the acts I do.

The humming bird

(From an observation before a funeral in
Michoacan, Mexico.)

Inside the old church all was still.
The midday light was so subdued
I could not clearly see what frill
beset the rugged cross I viewed.

Gorgeous artificial flowers
made of marble and of stone
fell to the Feet like summer showers
that want to worship and atone.

A humming bird whirred to a bloom,
seeking a nectar absent there
and finding nothing to consume
called on each flower in despair.

It flew in and out each chalice
as though it never would admit
that someone had the gall and malice
to make this charming counterfeit.

It hovered and then streaked away
to look for what its heart desired.
With nothing there it didn't stay
among the colors it admired.

For just a while it was deluded
by the splendor it perceived
yet quickly learned and concluded
that it was lies that he believed.

I thought how we, too, seek in things
where nothing ever satisfies
and to the foolish heart that climgs
becomes the way it ossifies.

It shocks me

It shocks me to realize
my every thought, word and deed
is the way I vandalize
the one I love, the one I need -
to find I stubbornly won't see
you suffer from my tyranny.

My sheer indifference is the sin.
My ignorance keeps you at bay
so that I won't pry within
to see how you suffer from my play -
behind the burden that I place
on the one whom I disgrace.

Since we are one you can't escape
the actions of my daily round.
It's your innocence I rape
your purity I defile and hound,
detouring your intentions so
that I dam them in their flow.

My sin is that I know and yet
the very wrongs that I instill
force the offspring that I beget
to soil and paralyze my will
decreeing that you share the bed
with each new evil that I bred.

When everyone is sleeping

When everyone is sleeping
and the dark is deep and still
my eager heart is leaping
to fuse into God's will.

Then I feel a bliss so warming
that my joy becomes complete
for the One that I am storming
gives Himself up in defeat.

Breakthrough

I have broken through my isolation
onto a new yet familiar terrain.
My heart sings in quiet elation
for I have escaped the inner strain
caused by defenses I have kept
and over which no one has stepped.

It was mySelf from which I was separated.
Life is one but its parts are endless
and this exclusion only generated
feelings that I'm alone and friendless
since behind my self-made partition
I lost the truth and its vision.

Now I reach out to both enemy and friend.
What joy there is in loving the hated,
when I no longer have to depend
on feelings that once segregated.
At last the unlovable has changed
because I no longer am deranged.

It was merely a point of view
in which the conscious mind indulged,
but once I had broken through
the truth became clearly divulged:
In God's own image everyone was made
that in our likeness His may be displayed.

The great dawning

For years I asked how "thou art I,"
and why I'm unaware of this,
and where this saving likeness is
that's so hard to identify.

How do you, Lord, think through my mind?
work through my hands? walk through my feet?
love through my heart all those I meet?
and serve when I serve humankind?

One day it clearly dawned on me.
I saw that when I do your will
with all my energy and skill
we melt in silent unity.

Then my will is not my own.
I have surrendered it to you,
and what I say and think and do
are now performed by you alone!

Dual role

What I call you is whom I am -
so my mind is telling me,
but my heart will not cram
the thought of you indwelling me.

It prefers the love it feels
of you visiting my soul,
and so it pretends and conceals
that it plays a dual role.

The dancing warrior

I'm fighting shadows in the dark,
flashes of light in the shining noon,
reflections that lead me off the mark
and offer only grief and pain as boon.
My sword clashes harshly to defeat
the apparitions I am forced to meet.

I dance over corpses of my dreams,
disgorging the demons of each desire,
while the lust that the flesh esteems
is flung into my dispassion's fire
'till it's enthroned on skulls and bones,
as Lords of all the skeletons he owns.

Yes, I am victor on this bloody field,
but no sooner do I come to turn around
than the corpses resurrect and yield
greater arms and begin to hound
and snap at my Achilles heel until
there's another legion that I must kill.

But I have learned to dance on death and pain,
and watch their defeat rise from the ashes,
once more to force them into dust again,
wounded by the fury of my clashes
only to find that which I so nobly fought
were merely phantoms of my own deluded thought.

You wake so gently

You wake so gently in my chest,
here where I meditate outside,
until I see each form is blessed,
a holy place where you abide.
Then I slowly melt in unity
with you and the world I see.

Your sweetness upholds everything.
That's why all creatures love to live.
Where you abound our lives do spring
into the joys and bliss you give
for you are the goal and the source
that leads our lives upon their course.

All your creatures feel with me
how you penetrate and sustain
and in your goodness deal with me
by mixing pleasure with my pain
to show me how I must chose
that which I must never lose.

And so my meditations bloom
and change into a living seed
in which there is no special room
for any isolated creed
that claims to be your only heir
when I can see you everywhere!

Imprint

It's in the marrow of my bones,
and in my genes and chromosomes
the fact that I have loved and known you!
It's in my flesh and every cell
in all my powers that impel
and even in the worship I have shown you.

    You are my Self, my life and being,
    the very universe that I am seeing.

It's in my taste and in my smell,
and in my dreams and hopes as well,
flowing through my veins with mighty force!
It's in my hearing and my sight,
in all I touch to my delight,
the very essence of my life and source.

    From your substance I was made,
    the one you then chose to invade.

Then to feel we're separated
is delusion generated,
for you are I and I am one with you.
But this estrangement seems
woven from fallacious dreams
which even makes the truth appear untrue.

    Your presence permeates me so
    that you are all that I can know:

    Grand, noble and ever freeing -
    and eternally imprinted on my being!

Wondering what freedom is

One night in my troubled dreams
I walked into a jail.
Behind the bars sat prisoners
all distraught and pale.
Some officers took finger prints,
some were on the 'phone
I stoood in my bewilderment
ignored and all alone
Wondering what freedom is.

I walked into an empty cell
and firmly shut the door.
No one even noticed
I had not been here before.
I sat inside my tiny cell
neglected and forlorn
with inmates looking through me
as though I had not been born
while wondering what freedom is.

Finally I opened up the door
and walked away.
No one even bothered asking
why I wished to stay,
but later there were headlines
about some crazy male
who came into the town
and locked himself up in the jail
while wondering what freedom is.

They speculated why he
did this thing and so did I.
When I woke up from this dream
I clearly realized why.
I was born unshackled and
to be part of the game
I made my problems prisons
with freedom as my aim
while wondering what freedom is.

I see that problems keep
most folk from being all alone.
They fear to step outside the game
to walk off on their own.
So they subtly enter prisons
determined not to see
that the door that shuts them in
has no lock or key,
and they're wondering what freedom is.

The daisy

One day I climbed a mountain top
to get away from mice and men,
so I could find a place to stop
and organize my thoughts again.

My path wound through the chaparral
where flowers bloomed in such array,
the hill looked like a carnival
of color in the bright noon day.

Then in the foliage I saw
a pile of human excrement
that some person long before
had left there as a testament.

And from the middle of the turd
a daisy grew in all its glory,
creating from the pure absurd
a legend of a success story.

It was beautiful and glorious
those golden petals opening wide,
a plant that's so victorious
its very source is sanctified.

The runaway

I run away yet there you are
blinking down from every star.
I turn elsewhere just to behold
all creatures patterned in your mold.

I close my eyes
but hear your sighs
in the quiet of my mind
until I find
that you abound
in every sound.

I seal my ears
but fragrance steers
my thoughts in your direction
wooing me with their affection.

The subtle odors that I smell
trap me with your potent spell.

I taste you in the fare I eat -
the sour, saline, bitter, sweet.
As I relish what I drink
you become the thought I think.

And when I fast
I am aghast
to feel you in the sun and rain,
veiled beneath my joy and pain.

When I suppress reason and feeling
my very heart and mind starts reeling
with your presence in my soul -
that just surrender can control.

It makes me tremble then to see
It's not you I'm running from! It's me!

Dream learning

I think I learn more from my dreams
than from the world when I'm awake.
Such unconscious knowledge seems
stronger in its ability to shake!
than merely in the waking state
when facts are hard to inculcate.

As I wake I know that I have changed.
Suddenly the misty scape is clear
with every attitude so rearranged
it's like facing a new frontier
for I then know that how I see
is what has changed anew in me.

You reach me in my dreams and sleep
where in a vision of the night
you speak your word that goes so deep
it fills my unknown world with light,
so that when I wake it echoes still
in the dark caverns of my will.

Which tells me you instruct within
where no one else can ever enter,
and it's from here that I begin
to function from a clearer center
that realizes you do only teach
where spoken words can never reach!

Four insights

1. I can't predict

I can't predict when you will come.
Each visit is an ever-new surprise,
although I must admit that some
are in answer to my anguished cries.
It's when you show up unexpectedly
that gratitude transports my heart
until it fills with ecstasy
my universe and every part.
Then there is nothing else to see!
Though I sit still I move so fast
that I overcome my every enemy
and am totally victorious at last,
for as long as you are within my soul
I am completely free and whole.

2. But when you leave!

But when you leave I am all alone,
fractured into many pieces of desire -
all which I crave to leave or disown
to reach the state to which I now aspire;
that of being consciously one with you,
not only for some time, but ever -
united in all that I can think and do
and which no pain or fear could sever.
But without this awareness I falter,
groping here or there for inner peace
that one could destroy or alter,
and which can only grow and increase
until we're so united that your will
absorbs mine in its eternal thrill.

3. Could I but realize

Could I but truly realize
you never came and never left,
and both states were but pious lies
to keep my empty heart bereft.
You can only seem to leave
so I may strive to rise above
the restless flesh that makes me grieve
but which I pamper with my love.
That I may know that you are I,
one, unbreakable and free,
and although the flesh may satisfy
it never did belong to me,
but is just delusion's scheme
to keep me captive in this dream.

4. When your bliss delights

When your bliss delights my soul
I am completely satisfied.
Then I am content and whole
for all my pain and fear have died.
Though I do nothing I have all.
Though only here I'm everywhere.
The joy you give can so enthrall
no other pleasure can compare!
Then in your Self I find my own
for it's in you that I now live,
and it is you and you alone
that I receive and which I give
since everything that I now see
has you as only destiny.

Ma Durga

You were always there for me!
Someone to love, guide and protect me,
who proved that you did care for me
when the furies come to dissect me.

You were everything God seemed to be -
not almighty, omnipresent and all-knowing -
but full of gentleness, love and humility
and a patient kindness that set me glowing.

Your example showed me what life is all about -
a steady growth from bad to good on to perfection.
Your words and counsels were self-controlled throughout;
your discipline so full of hidden smiles and affection
that in these expressions and attitudes I saw
what fills both gods and angels with great awe!

    The rainbow's end

    How easy it's to give in
    and hard for us to fight.
    We want rainbows to live in
    and dream away the light.

    It is the flesh we battle
    when its lust force us to act
    until our minds just rattle
    and our energies are sacked.

    Yet all the while we're clinging
    to a skeleton of clay
    and take the pain it's bringing
    as reward for when we pray!

    At last when death has claimed us
    from the role each one esteems,
    we find out life has framed us
    with nothing but our dreams.

The imposter

I listen for your silence in my soul
but all I hear are noises of my thought,
those little selves my lust had wrought.
They have decided to take control
and stop me from reaching my own goal
of dancing with you in my solitude
above the thunder of my craving and its brood.

My battle cry is lost within the din
and clamor of my own restless desires,
impelling me to cast off my discipline
and enjoy the music of my senses lyres
to which my flesh lewdly aspires,
not wanting to see that I'm lead astray
by each game I create and chose to play.

I am confronted with the disturbing fact:
there is a dark usurper lurking deep within,
who makes me feel that I have always lacked
the reckless joy that comes from wanton sin
when one wrestles with another skin to skin,
but furtively ignoring that this impostor
feeds on these mis-emotions that I foster.

Intruder

Intruder in a no-man's land,
with nothing it can understand.
An alien in its own home town,
an amnesiac acting like a clown,
who guesses he lived here before
but finds no landmarks anymore.
Like a bad B-movie it's all untrue
but it does leave me with one clue:
a puppet that's pulled on a string
that knows how but does not want to sing,
and mouths the words for a voice,
a role in which it had no choice,
someone brought back from the dead
but with a stranger in its head.

The glow of sin

We err beneath the lure of sin,
fall into its embrace with ease
because there is this urge within
to follow what we think will please.
We're blinded by its tempting glow
that dupes the heart so it can't know
it's there to trick us and to tease.

We ignore it as the subtle lie
and cling to it while being burned,
and foolishly keep wondering why
we reap the crop we haven't earned,
unaware that the joys that we pursue
is just a clever counterfeit of you -
a fact which we have not discerned.

We live by sin's deceiving rules
since we forgot what we must see:
that we are just delusion's fools,
all jailed in pleasure's agony
whereas we're so magnificent and grand
that the world can never understand
sin mimics you but cannot set us free.

The geranium

A beautiful geranium grew
from a chamber pot on a wall
but I bet it never knew
what hemmed in its roots at all.

It blossomed gladly in the sun
to spread its generosity
so as to challenge everyone
to live without pomposity.

Empty dreams

How bleak the scene that we behold
when our wills are emasculated,
and one by one our dreams unfold
the emptiness they generated.

Without a goal we're doomed to perish.
Without a dream we live in vain
but everything we're taught to cherish
we see at last with great disdain.

The world's ideas are only pipe dreams
that betray us when they burst,
and are life's archetype schemes
to control us with our thirst.

All our ambitions were just bait
to hook us to this fickle show
where we endure the bitter fate
of empty dreams that we outgrow.

When I drift

When I drift without direction
it's because I've lost sight of you,
living my life in subjection
to some past mental residue.

But you won't let me flow away.
You chase me down into my soul
where either I submit or pay
by running out of self-control.

You are a habit I can't break,
someone I know so intimately and well
that any excursion into sin I take

confines me to that inner hell
where my thoughts are so compressed
all I can be is self-obsessed.

Not knowing

I find it impossible to understand
what any part of life is all about.
When I think I have some command
I'm flung onto a totally different route
where I realize what I know isn't so
and what I seek's not there to know.

Suddenly my ignorance tells me
that day after day I know less and less,
and that the wisdom society sells me
are lies that I must dispossess,
sensing what they know is just a dream
whereas its waking knowledge that I must esteem.

Now I am awake from the great lie
but the truth still hides its face,
and though I seek and pray and pry
I find only a glimmer or a trace
that forces me to realize
that all I know is otherwise.

String bound

Like a kite my heart soars high
into the winds to sail the clouds
where I am free to ride the sky
and float above the weary crowds.
Though I flutter so high above
a busy world I see and love,
something in me won't let go
to higher states I yearn to know.
With just enough freedom to roam
in altitudes where I can dance
with other kites that I romance,
I dare to call the sky my home,
but as long as I am string bound
I still belong down on the ground.

The movie Show

My life seems like a movie show,
a dream from which I am awake,
but which I still can't overthrow
caught in the mem'ry of its ache,
where beyond my imagination
it shines like an hallucination.

At times I feel so damned detached
that only I seem to exist,
the world an idea that I had hatched
to entertain this lone monist
who sometimes still sees the dream
as something that he must redeem.

Not wide awake, nor deep asleep!
I step in and outside of this play
where demons laugh and angels weep
as fantasies slowly decay
to find what I believe and see
are my own dreams deceiving me.

Your holiness

In the quiet of my soul I feel
your holiness engulfing me,
evoking within me the zeal
to stay within your sanctity.

Then heaven fills my inner space.
I do not have to go and die
for with this knowledge comes your grace -
to bless the heart you occupy.

>Then does it matter who I am?
>or what I am? or where I am?
>or how I am? if all I am
>is what you will for me!

This is how your holiness is mine!
and, oh!, the joy and bliss you share
anoints my life with love divine
and happiness beyond compare.

Four new insights

1. Behind my thoughts

Behind my thoughts you wait for me.
I feel you although my mind strays,
for I have ceased to create for me
the fear of living in this maze.
You are with me in this jail!
and can't escape it on your own,
for no matter how high the bail
I will not pay for it alone.
You flow through me and around me
and with me in the core of my joy,
and even if pain comes to hound me
it arrives to teach and not destroy,
thus making me aware that you
are always present in the acts I do.

2. Since we are one

Since we are one how can you avoid
feeling my suffering and confusion?
For oneness means nothing's destroyed
but felt in common without exclusion!
The reason that I can't feel you
is that my own imperfections hide
what you are in the very wrongs I do
especially when I act out of pride.
But you do not have this recourse
and must feel everything I undergo.
My thoughts and feelings reinforce
what my mind did not want to know:
that when I sin you must endure
the evils that my acts procure!

3. Evil is manifest in sin

It shows that evil is manifest in sin!
for what you are appears to be degraded,
and since you are the guest within
with my performance you're abraded.
My very thoughts and deeds pollute you
when my free will sports alone,
and my decisions all refute you
when they're created on their own.
This consciousness that we share
is debased when I transgress
for you are forced to be coheir
of its results and distress,
suffering through me its effect
when my peace and joy are wrecked.

4. Your native state

Since freedom is your native state
you're concerned with our liberty
because you are caught in a strait,
co-suffering our agony.

Because this free choice that you gave
is the problem that underlies
the way we're trained to behave
but which we do not recognize.

This gift of free will has the force
to make your values seem unreal,
while you won't give yourself recourse
to break in us its self-appeal.

Therefore our wills keep yours enjailed,
trapped in the heart where you abide,
and your freedom is so curtailed
its life is almost nullified.

Is it you, Lord?

Is it you, Lord, who have slipped
in between my thoughts and feelings?
With whom I have fellowshipped
unbeknownst in all my dealings?

Whose quietness fills my breast
and expands my heart, including
the way to solve each sudden test
even when it is deluding?

It is you who lift me up
as the ocean holds the wave,
but come to share and sup
even when I misbehave!

Who else could it be but you!
for whom I am is just you sporting,
living your life through what I do,
my very self that you're supporting;

Who plays as I, seemingly all apart,
but actually dwells deep within me,
not just as a presence in my heart
but who is my real identity.

The unexpected

I find you when I least expect it.
You open like a blossom in my soul
to wake it from its sleep and resurrect it
as joy peals out like Easter bells that toll.

I feel you bursting through my senses,
your sweetness infusing its bliss in me
and my mind shudders and untenses
when it surrenders to your kiss in me.

Then there is no human time and space,
or boundaries that can restrict me.
No ideas or concepts that can debase
or with their promises addict me!
Only you in which I am then so complete
that what I used to be has become obsolete.

Running free

I've been running free my whole life long,
yet actually believing that I'm in a jail
and that I am in fact tormented by a song
which rhymes and rhythms make me fail.

   It's with these thoughts that life controls me,
   with my feelings that I'm bound and lead,
   with such ideas that life consoles me,
   while I move along the living dead.

I have believed the theories I've been taught,
lies that are perpetrated as truth or fact,
deceptions that my childish mind has bought
but by which my foundations have been sacked.

   Yet I've bought into this lie by being born,
   by the programmed need to truly belong
   but from which I have earned only scorn
   when my truth was condemned as wrong.

I was born freer than any thought or feeling,
freer than the wind, a bird, a cloud or beast
and the only thing that truly can set me reeling
is when I mingle in my mind society's yeast.

   It is better to drop out than stay in,
   It is better to disappear from their scene,
   It is better to lose than to lie and win
   than live in a place that's never been.

Now I dance in galaxies and nebulae
to a cosmic music that the atoms all vibrate,
a beat no feet can stamp, no voice portray,
through which angelic laughters percolate.

   And all prisons and confinements are forgotten
   as the self dances in the Self with exultation
   and those nightmares are now seen as miss-begotten
   and demolished in the bliss of meditation.

Free choice or not

It took me sixty-six long years to see
that I'm the master of my choices
and that it's with this mystery
that I create my endless voices.
I forge the path I'm forced to take
with the decisions that I make.

But my mind is ruled by like and disdain.
So my choices are not made without sway
but still conditioned by pleasure and pain
that influence my options in a subtle way.
Thus my "free choice" seems just a notion
that my wish fulfillment set in motion.

Yet a wrong decision is better than none
because resolutions do assign a course
that brings into perspective each phenomenon
as it casts a light upon its source.
Then in hindsight one can clearly find
that free choice or not, decisions shape a mind.

Liberty

You took me at my word
and truly stripped me bare
to show me just how absurd
it's to live in daydreams anywhere.
Those ideals I so adored
were really chains that bound me tight
in a nightmare I abhorred
but ruled me harshly with my fright.
Though my freedom has no place
it permeates all of my mind
where I cannot find a trace
of what used to keep me blind
for once dreams were stripped from me
all that remained was liberty.

Always the same

Behind my thoughts and feelings
    I am always the same.
Behind my wheelings and dealings
    I am always the same.
Time changes its hours but!
    I am always the same.
And space expands its powers but
    I am always the same.
Yesterday, today and tomorrow
    I am always the same.
In joy and bliss and sorrow
    I am always the same.
Like the sun that never sets
    I am always the same.
Like the rain that ever wets
    I am always the same.
For like the One who made me
    I am always the same.
Even when delusions invade me
    I am always the same.

But when I forget this fact
    that's when I begin to act
like a soul who thinks it changes
    and so enters delusion's ranges
that only has one simple aim,
    to prove that I am not the same
beneath all surfaces and externals
    and so denies the real eternals.

Yet while they stand and rave at me
    denying my own true identity
I find no matter what they claim
    the truth is: I'm always the same.

Christ time

The blossoms burst out through the sand,
quivering in the desert breeze,
shooting colors into the land
as though to laugh and tease,
saying that beneath their cover
hides spring which is their lavish lover.

Was it spring that was breaking through?
for from the flowers beams of light
burst through their roots, giving a clue
that Christ was flaring into my sight
as life and shape, color and spring,
the hidden music all forms sing.

Christ was playing here as flowers,
falling from the clouds as rain,
thundering his power showers
as lightning tore the sky in twain
till I was sure that all is he,
unraveling his mystery.

My lips began to sing his praise,
my heart in love with his whole being,
my soul exalting in a craze
with the presence I was seeing,
a presence that excludes no one
from being what he is: God's Son!

My only sin

I'm neither here, nor am I there!
Not in darkness, and not in light.
Nor in hope or sheer despair,
not in jail, neither in flight . . .
Just drifting, floating, merely bobbing
with a heart that's scarcely throbbing.

What has happened to this child?
Is this the Hyde that I've become?
my way of being tame, not wild
and life a mission burdensome?
Someone so anesthetized
his every feeling's cauterized?

Yet in this drifting state I grope.
Not in pain, neither in pleasure.
Just someone who has lost all hope
and any dream that he can measure,
with longing so far left behind
he's disconnect from humankind.

But below this vacuous state
I hear you whisper in my ear
that it never is too late
to fight until I persevere
and that I only have one sin:
the cowardice of giving in.

I lie around

I lie around to my surprise,
and yet I act more than I think,
eschewing the need to theorize
here where I'm standing on the brink
of pure nothing and contentment,
enjoying for once a self-relentment.

Is this a laziness that I examine?
Still, if it's so, I don't seem to care
for in my heart there is no famine
of having to go anywhere.
I'm now enjoying just a state
of satisfaction inviolate.

> Yet there is always a teasing doubt
> as to what my life is all about,
> and I wonder at my fragile treasure
> is not just a passing pleasure.
>
> Am I just lying to myself again?
> to ease my conscience and its pain?
> or is this gloriously true
> that I know that I am one with you?

But as I self-analyze
I find the facts are all the same.
I've seen through your disguise
and know now that you claim my name.
Except for this form I wear
I find no difference anywhere!

Come to me

In the quiet of the morning
while peace is still adorning
a muted world engrossed in sleep
and silence reigns supreme and deep
Come to me!

Reveal yourself to me this day.
Teach me to follow in your way.
Let your will be done so you
are glorified in all I do.
Come to me!

If the hustle of my action
breeds a false satisfaction
let me feel that you are wooing
me in all that I am doing.
Come to me!

My mind is calling, pleading, yearning.
My heart's entreating, trembling, burning.
My will is searching, reaching, bending.
My soul is longing without ending.
Come to me!

In the stillness of the night
when sentience has taken flight
and dense obscurity reveals
what day disguises and conceals
Come to me!

In the absence of desire
fan my love as I aspire
and experience my essence
glowing in your incandescence.
Come to me!

And at that moment when I'm dying
from a world so mystifying
I'll cry out my last farewell
as I leave my fleshly citadel:
You've come to me!

No more self-lynching

Fighting all my thoughts are worse
than battling hordes of Saracen.
At least they die or disperse
but my thoughts resurrect again
as they venture to profane
my spirit on its own terrain.

It's my own mind that I battle
where I fight myself victoriously
and my forces shake and rattle
when ideas strike vaingloriously,
forcing me to live and obey
those precepts that lead me astray.

No more, O God! No more, I cry.
Enough of forcing down my urges
which I can only mollify
when my imagination splurges
but leaves me so wrenched in two
I feel outraged and torn from you.

No more of this inner lynching!
this endless self-depreciation!
that sends me retching, squirming, flinching
in persistent self-alienation
just because I cannot be
what I surmise you want from me!

Drugged by dreams

Drugged by dreams that anesthetize,
thoughts that create a false contentment,
ambitions that eventually penalize
and shape in the heart a rude resentment,
lulled and mislead, dulled and unsaid,
I live a life which I now dread.

Because I look out from the five senses
and seek a meaning the world bestows,
but in spite of all my pretenses
my heart rebels for it knows
the world's allure is fantasies and lies
that it bestows as its greatest prize.

It's within the soul's deepest layers
that you dwell as the unknown witness,
and see that my dreams are the slayers
and how I judge my worth and fitness
whereas you are the real foundation
from which my desires seek confirmation.

So unless I give up these lies I die
even while I claim victory and success.
My dreams can fruitfully multiply
only when you're their source and happiness,
but to claim the urges of the flesh alone
is to rule upon a straw and empty throne.

I have stopped reaching

I have stopped my inner reaching,
the struggle to be anchored in you,
that continuous inner beseeching
which helped me triumph as I withdrew
from the world and its attraction
which never gave me satisfaction.

But in doing so I became stale.
Something is now stilted within me
so that all my efforts only fail
as I'm straight-jacketed in misery.
I don't belong in any place and time,
bled dry and shriveled in my prime.

And now I stretch out a withered hand,
hoping you'll heal me without delay
but some inner reason makes me understand
that it's with my effort that I must pay
and crawl out of this self-dug pit
to help me give up self-will and submit.

Yet something in me objects and claims
that once one has fallen one can't rise
but that is the sin which truly frames
the heart to become and remain unwise,
for falling is not so much a grievous sin
but it is remaining there by giving in.

Veiled in pain

Our universe is veiled in pain
where pleasure pacifies our rage
but suffering's built into our grain
and ties us to the body's cage
in which we strive to find a balm
that will bring us instant calm.

We won't believe life is a dream
that punishes us with hopes of power,
and that its promise can't redeem
when it is programmed to devour
not only the mind with its hopes
but the way with which it copes.

The world we know is made to grind
us down until nothing is left,
and we are compelled to find
that our beliefs are all so deft
they make us rationalize and say
that there can be no other way!

But behind pleasure and pain,
and all duality there lies
a state that cannot wax or wane.
It is the very fabric of our cries,
and when we merge into its presence
eternal joy becomes our essence.

Just to be

Just to be without having to prove -
not having to justify or to achieve;
to establish my claim and then to move
in a manner I was taught to believe.
Just to be, Oh God, just to be
what it is meant to be just me.

Just not having to attain any goal
or to feel that I have to serve,
and to live only with inner control
to evoke all the joy I deserve!
Not to do because I have to or should
or because this might be for my good;

Just to be because I am me!
Without contributing a thing,
and to feel so disgustingly free
that I can cry out and sing,
and to be the only one of my kind
in a way no one ever opined.

Just to be, Oh God! just to be;
with no delusions to lead me astray
and to feel freedom flowing from me,
blessing all creatures in my way -
a child out of bondage, a child out of jail!
released from a program that trained me to fail.

Who you are

I'm tired of the answers I create,
thinking they must come from you,
since circumstances all negate
what my desires misconstrue.
I hear only what I crave to hear
and am so deaf to what you say
that if you truly should appear
I'll just tell you to go away.
Because you're not what I project -
only what you yourself reveal to me,
and I see I must not even expect
what any experience of you will be
for my anticipations will conceal
the truth it seeks with its own zeal.

Winter's price

There seems a glimmer in the dark,
or is it just a memory of light
that comes to taunt me with its spark
and verify the eternalness of night?

I hear running water where all was still,
ice melting to form a living stream,
telling me that the cold night will
end to wake me from this frigid dream.

Is it a breeze against my frozen cheek?
a thaw in the numbing, biting chains
or is it that my wind is weak
and wants to end its gnawing pains?

Is there a promise of a coming day
that can't stop the sun from shining?
or perhaps a bold and new sadistic way
to make sure my heart keeps pining?

And yet I swear I feel a new mood rise,
spring time pressing up against the ice
that forces me anew to realize
that spring is worth the winter's price.

In the silence

In the silence I sense you're near.
There is a sweet vastness in my chest.
Any moment now you might appear
as my sole love, my glorious guest.

There is a hearing in my feeling.
No words, but the messages are plain.
It's no fantasy with which I'm dealing
that I am functioning on your terrain.

Your sweetness has become my very own.
Your joy flows freely through my soul
as the bliss that you and you alone
can give me in this novel role,
for as you speak your power is conferred
so that I too become your spoken word.

The surprise

Each moment of my life is a surprise!
I'm gripped in habits, trapped and bound
when suddenly I come to realize
the chains lay strewn upon the ground.

Astonishment and marvel is how
I feel in hindsight when I find
you freed me not here and now
but when all hope fled from my mind.

Lest I should think I did the act -
that my pride would swell out of hand,
you healed me when I knew I lacked
the way to do so at my command.

This is why you amaze me so!
When I find each day I am more free
for it's only then I come to know
it's you who give me liberty!

He is I

I found you in my ebb and flow -
so tenuous it took me years to realize
that the one I craved to know
is the force behind my cries.

Silently you slid in my emotions
and the flesh from which they've sprung
and which pulse enforced my motions
that this grace was left unsung.

O Lord for whom I was yearning,
all the time you were waiting,
listening how my thoughts were churning
the love that I was so creating.

My expectations of what you should be
denied me access to your presence.
Through my projections I couldn't see
that everywhere is your quintessence.

Then once I called on you again
and found a joy so thrilling me
that it eradicated all my pain
to become my constant ecstasy.

To my great surprise I found
that consciousness which always is,
flowing everywhere I look around
as an everlasting inner bliss.

So gentle, humble, hidden and still -
that even then I could not accept
that it was you who felt me thrill
and for whom I yearned and wept.

Oh, he is I! Yes, he is I!
The one for whom I yearned is me!
So close it is no wonder why
it took so long for me to see.

A song of freedom

You've set me free and now I sing
a song that I have never learned,
but which to my delight does bring
a joy that I have never earned.

Such words of freedom fill my brain
I even rejoice in my sleep.
It leads me far beyond all strain
to where you bliss within my deep.

It is your rhythm ever flowing
through all time and space in me,
and leads wherever I am going
to dance the dance of liberty.

Sounding gently everywhere
its theme pulsates my every thought,
going before me to prepare
a life I never could have bought.

An only son

Only you can blend my will
lastingly into your own,
and so tranquilize and still
my restlessness for you alone.
Outside your will is hell and pain
of a life that's lived in vain.

Only you can fuse my soul
into union with you.
I have made you my goal
in all I think and do.
Open now the springs of grace
that I may see you face to face.

Only you can now capture me
as your love flows from within
my being to so enrapture me
that it burns out every sin,
for when your will makes us one
I too become an only son.

No objection

I don't know where I'm going
and the way remains unclear,
with not one step showing
the path away from here.
Everything changes so fast
I don't know what to do
for what enticed me in the past
now leads away from you.

Like a love affair that's ended
the flame died and in its stead
a lonely darkness has descended
that keeps me stranded in its dread.
All I feel is fear and regret
for what has changed in me so fast
and under which spell I met
my own dark side at last.

This is what I would not know,
the facts I feared to face,
going where I dread to go
and which steps I can't retrace.
Against my will I drift away,
unable to resist or grieve
but that you just let me stray
I find the hardest to believe.

Free choice or not, I do not care!
Why do you let me on my own
when I don't know how to repair
my way back to you alone?
Life changed and I'm out of control,
drifting in an unknown direction
but what shocks me is your role
of not voicing your objection!

I sought for meaning

I sought for meaning and found none.
Purpose did not exist for me,
and in all the things that I have done
significance would not persist for me.

I looked for you in outer places,
hoping activities and goals would give
direction and hidden, secret graces
to illuminate how I should live.

But I felt abandoned and betrayed.
Life itself gave me no true design,
and even though I sacrificed and prayed
I worshipped in an empty shrine.

One day I found to my joy and shock:
You are the relevance I always sought,
and that you alone can unlock
the intent veiled behind my thought.

You are the meaning I now find.
Everything else is a decoy
to deceive the restless mind
from knowing you're its only joy!

Wearied

I am wearied with talk and chatter,
voices that nag at me and natter
about things that don't really matter.

I want to hear what silence is saying
and the music which stillness is playing
and hide in the pauses while I am praying.

Just to be alone without words to flay me,
evoking emotions that always betray me
as they propel dreams that are born to slay me.

Give me silence in which nothing arises,
filled with quietness' greatest surprises:
joy in which love specializes.

Just let me rest

Lord, I am tired and crave peace.
Just let me rest in your rapture.
I seek that calmness and release
which I myself cannot capture.
For once let me be completely whole
beyond the world and its control.

God, I want to vomit right out
all the grossness of the world
in which I have grovelled about
and in which all my goals were hurled
but in the end betrayed me so
that there is nowhere I can go.

Even my hope in you now seems in vain.
When I think I feel that we are one
I forget all my fear and pain
but now this state's become undone
leaving me alone and rejected
since you, my joy, have defected.

Just let me rest from all this striving
so that my mind be anesthetized and soothed,
and giving up this relentless driving
from everything that I want proved,
so that when I come to myself once more
I'll find it's merely dreams that I abhor.

The door

Why don't you open when I knock?
You must be home since you are everywhere,
but your door is under key and lock,
making it seem that you don't care.

I call but silence mutes my sound
as I pray that you must come to me!
but I feel your indifference abound
stressing my own uncertainty.

Yet I find gifts in unexpected places;
presents that can only come from you -
quiet, hidden and those subtle graces
that are revealed in the things I do.

There's peace where there was none before!
Are you not the very peace I sought?
No more battles in life's endless war
when love sports in my every thought.

Then I realize that you do come to me.
Not in the form of the Lord that I expect
but as virtues that increase my liberty
and fill my soul to make it resurrect.

Now I knock and in the knocking wait.
This time how will you respond to me?
As your door opens to my life and fate
you come unseen as my own sanctity.

Born outside

I was born outside and the night was cold.
I was born outside while the thunder rolled
and my cry got lost in the wind and the rain
as it echoed far over hill and plain.

I was born outside as the night wind's child.
I was born outside and my heart is wild.
You can hear my call in a dream or a vision,
catch a glimpse of me like an apparition.

I'm a clansman to the thunder,
the lightning, wind and rain
with whom I dance in wonder
to a mystical refrain.

You can join me in the sunrise
where I flicker like a star
and sing in sheer surprise
when you find me where you are!

I was born outside in this wild frontier.
I was born outside just to coax you near
so we both can be like a song that's free
as we race through time to eternity.

From the sea roar I will call you
to remind you who you are.
Through sunsets that enthrall you
I will beckon from afar.

At daybreak I will leave you
to think you only dreamed
while others will deceive you
and say that you blasphemed.

I was born outside, just to lure you home.
I was born outside that you cease to roam
and we'll always be just two together
birds of a kind, of a golden feather.

I was born outside . . . way outside . . .
Far outside . . . just to lure you home.

The omnipresent heart

Right now I radiate your love.
It's glowing like a gentle fire
that warms from below and above,
and draws me inwards and higher
to where you're filling everything
with love like an eternal spring.

I then perceive that you have made
the universe and all its creatures
out of your Self; that you pervade
what I behold in all its features,
delighting that it's right and true:
no thing exists apart from you!

We're all contained within your being!
No one is good or evil in your sight.
Our free choice is how we're decreeing
by claiming what is wrong or right.
It is like and dislike that makes
the foolish heart suffer mistakes.

Now as I view creation I can see
how your love pervades and activates.
My soul expands in ceaseless ecstasy
as it embraces and vibrates
to include the whole and every part
of your omnipresent heart!

I recognize you

It's not in bells or lights
that I recognize when you're here;
not in imagination's inner flights
when in majesty you may appear!
Not in fragrance or a lovely sound,
or in exaggerated feelings that inspire,
or in great insights where you abound
but in the conquest of desire.

When they no longer can compel
and doing your will is the only goal
and thoughts or words can never tell
of the quietness within my soul;
and happiness blooms gently where
deep peace borders on a joyous calm,
I know you as the sweetness that I share
and lay on as a healing balm.

I recognize you in serenity and peace.
This is how you manifest in me,
and it's from this state that you increase
to mold me into sanctity.
You are the sweetness I then feel,
the warmth and stillnesses that nourish
for this love and joy that you reveal
is your own bliss in which I flourish.

Dance eternal

One night I dreamed my master came
and with his love set me aflame.
He said, "I've come that we may sup
and you, my friend, may share my cup."

I gazed into his eyes of bliss
and knew that I was ever his.
I merged with him and he with me
'till he was my identity.

Then his heart came from his chest,
exchanging hearts within my breast.
And as I felt his ecstacy
he gently said, "Come, dance for me!"

And then I danced exultantly -
I drunk with him and he with me.
And as I yielded all control
he took possession of my soul.

I felt him dancing through my being.
My feet were light and ever fleeing,
charged with a rhythm of their own,
alone, but never quite alone.

I danced through fire, snow and rain,
through sleep and dreams, pleasure and pain.
I danced through valleys, cities, seas,
deserts, mountains, grass and trees.

Through the present, future and past,
and kingdoms that would never last.
And as I danced my wisdom grew
for he was all I saw and knew.

And all the time I felt him near
since perfect love had cast out fear.
His love had bound us ever one -
two hearts that throbbed in unison.

I woke up to his happy beat
for he's still dancing through my feet,
where his pulse goes on because
I'm always dancing to his laws.

The wall of dreams

Every dream imprisons us except
the one we skirt, that leads to you.
All others keep our wills inept
with the illusions they accrue,
lusts with which our minds create
the visions with which we mismate
but that we so ardently pursue.

Dreams are but the world's decoy
that hide the truth behind their lure
and which quietly erodes our joy
until there is no hope or cure,
for that which fails to reveal you
is consciously made to conceal you
so that our wisdom always stays impure.

But the dream to do your will
gives to others their direction
and safely guides our hearts until
we have made the great connection
where every dream is truly seen
as a wall that's built between
God and the soul that seeks perfection.

The smile of God

In the quiet of my meditation
when restless thoughts disappeared
and feelings were beyond frustration
and the confusion that they reared;
as I sat there without guile
suddenly I felt your smile!

At first I was full of wonder
as it was delighting me,
but then I thought I was under
some delusion that was inciting me
to think that I was so good
I already had reached sainthood.

All at once I was smiling too!
My face became alive and beaming
and I knew for sure that you
smiled in my soul. I wasn't dreaming,
only aware this smile was yours
that radiated through my pores.

I went so deep there was no space,
no time or human point of view!
only awareness without place -
a state you let me share with you
as you let me feel for a while
the miracle of your own smile!

In you I live

In you I live.
How warm and safe your being.
The very joy that you give
is fulfilling and so freeing
that fear evaporates in fear
when I know that you are near,
so near in me
that I melt in happiness,
finding out that I be
your being that's expressed as bliss.

You lure me deep within
where I'm denuded of all sin -
at least for the time that we
are in will-united ecstasy.

And when it seems that you leave
my astonished heart can only grieve,
even though it knows that you
are what it is and loves to woo.

Victim Soul
(For Marno McCarley)

Christ is hanging on the cross through you,
and when you offer him your agony and pain
from your sufferings, he can then accrue
a living grace to convert the lost and vain.
Your flesh becomes an altar through which he
is offered as a victim for all sinners.
Your illness is not futile and will be
a force to transform losers into winners.
Then in your own hidden and humble way
you are one with him who reaches out for souls
and no force in time or space can convey
what such a willing sacrifice extols -
for suffering in and with him you must rise
to share the glory of his eternal paradise.

Amapola

A tidal wave of yellow hit my gaze
as amapolas danced beneath the sun.
A flower cascade with an urgent craze
to make each moment count before its done.

My companion said that this plant
contains a cruel and addictive drug
whose very nature it is to enchant
before it turns into a thug.

Dance, amapola, dance! Enjoy the summer wind.
You don't know that you contain a curse.
When we consume your being we have sinned
by using you to make our natures worse.

You activate in us our greed and lust,
clinging to what we think gives us power,
but which only drives us into the dust
that we grind out of your own flower.

You dance and sway so bright and merrily!
Your face flashing its yellow smiles
and if I were told there is only one to see
I would gladly go and walk a thousand miles.

The face

Behind a flimsy veil the face
of which I used to dream in fright,
that made my mind a haunted place,
abandoned and deprived of light.

Yet there it hung before a door,
the only way of reaching you,
but I could only stoop before
what fear kept me from passing through.

I cringed at what I thought I'd see,
because I knew it was alive
and would claw and mangle me
so that I never could survive.

I tried in anguish to subdue
the fear that forced me to recoil
but every effort would renew
and aggravate my own turmoil.

But in a dream I crushed my awe
and tore the veil from its throne.
I gasped at shock at what I saw:
the face I dreaded was my own!

It was just a picture drawn
on a young and fertile mind,
and was made to vex and spawn
fears to keep me weak and blind.

But as I studied it with care
my startled heart began to race
for slowly I became aware
that from my looks emerged Christ's face.

The no-place

Deep in the caverns of my being,
beyond all thoughts, words and deeds,
or what fantasies may be decreeing
or the program of ancestral seeds
there is a state that has no place -
just flawless love and joy and grace.

Eyes can't see where this may be.
Ears can't hear its silent voice,
but touch can feel its ecstasy
as it surrenders to rejoice
that from this vast and empty state
all forms and names originate.

This is what fills the heart with bliss,
the will with power, the night with light;
from which there flows an endless genesis
that gives us name and form and sight,
an empty point from which arrives
the dual playground of our lives.

And when I sink into its conscious deep
I find it is my Self that I then feel,
beyond waking, dreams and profound sleep,
what intellect or mind cannot reveal -
where what I am is so vast and un-designed
that what I'm not is how I am defined.

When hell is over

When hell's over and heaven begins,
how can I ever explain its glory?
When the hare races and the tortoise wins,
who will believe the story?

'Till yesterday I was caught in a net
of such inward agony and pain
I thought I'd never stop to fret
or ever normalize again.

But last night in forgotten dreams
your waters flowed to change my fate.
My pain was rushed away in streams
to places dark and desolate.

My heart blossomed in contemplation,
the desertscape flooded with bliss
until I was filled with such elation
I knew that this is what God is.

The gap between us

The gap between us has disappeared.
It's completely closed in meditation
when the Self in me is so revered
I'm lost within its exaltation.
I don't hear your music but become it.
My heart is hands with which I play it
but it is really you as I who strum it
so that my soul rejoices to relay it.
In the non-duality of inner quiet
when there's just awareness everywhere,
and this inner bliss is my only diet
then I know you have invaded my prayer -
that I have died and am so resurrected
that what I am is only you perfected.

Slay this little self

Slay this little self of mine
that there be solely you in me
and only that which be divine
may wound my heart with ecstasy.

Society I thought a friend
became a Judas in disguise
that betrayed me in the end
by veiling you, my greatest prize!

Oh, let this world turn as it will.
I ask for nothing more than this:
that you take my heart and fill
it with your everlasting bliss.

For then it will be only you
who exists disguised as me,
although in what I'll say and do
it's really you the world will see.

Within your silence

Within your silence is a satisfaction
that so thrills me there is no need
to go out and fill my time with action
from which my detours all proceed.

There is only a stillness that nourishes,
that ravishes with joy and such delight
my inner world expands and flourishes
when you are all that's in my sight.

And in this calmness I crave to remain;
not to escape from a time that is mad,
or to avoid things that cause me pain
and force me to be a lone nomad,
but simply to explore this inner state
from where all states originate.

A time bomb

A time bomb's ticking deep in me
to blow up all my old foundations
and release ideas that sleep in me,
to taunt me with their revelations.
I feel the pressure slowly rise,
a tension seeking its release
from thought patterns that brutalize
my inner world with sheer caprice.
And all I do is sit and wait
for the dread moment to arrive
unless some force will detonate
the threat so I can stay alive,
which may just be a greater curse
than the death I now rehearse.

Confusion

My problem is still undefined.
I believe you are its key
but the answer shy's my mind
and darkens its own mystery.

I must solve what I don't know
and blindly grope as I decode
a riddle I can't see although
I'm not supposed to leave the road.

I must love that which hides from me
and very seldom shows a face,
but always fades or strides from me
to leave me senseless in my place.

But my self-control still fails
whatever now the reason be
and I am full of self-betrayals
which terrorize and treason me.

And while you seem so far away
I think that you make me aware
that though I have nothing to say
my confusion is my prayer.

The stripping

I see nothing in or outside
for I'm cast off like a drone.
There is nothing, I confide,
that I can handle on my own,
for each goal, ambition and desire
has been nothinged in your fire.

Stripped of every wish and dream
and humbled to the point of ache,
I have nothing to redeem
so that I can finally awake!
I live a nightmare that destroys
all my inner peace and joys.

For in a nothingness I grope,
praying not to fall or stumble
as I trudge on without a hope,
biting my tongue not to grumble
for with my branches all so bare
I'm chilled to the bone in raw despair.

Oh, tear me down and break my pride
until this ego is controlled,
and I, at last, am free inside
if only just to be paroled -
because I know you will increase
when you strip me down to peace.

Hallucinations

The flesh can't give us anything
except more acute suffering,
while the mind is just a screen
through which our lives are seen -
until the bewildered soul
is totally under its control;
its life just another tale
of innocent prisoners in a jail,
who in their deluded misery
believe that they are truly free . . .
and that this life spells all
on a long, graffitied wall
where the slogans still deny
any act that will defy
a society that is truly drugged
and by its own hallucinations mugged!

The turtle dove

The turtle dove coos in sorrow
from a grimy, dusty cage
and he hopes that in the morrow
he'll wake free from this outrage.
Our little town is fast asleep.
Not even roosters crow the time,
but the dove's awake to weep
and bewail this heedless crime.
And as I listen to his grief
I want to share his smothered pain
and bring the feathered heart relief,
and say that he'll be free again
once he accepts and loves the source
that tortures him without remorse.

Groping

I grope along and wonder why
I can never find the way,
when my pain still turns awry
and I always seem to stray,
forcing me to divine and guess
my way through its deceptiveness.

How easy it would be for me
if I were programmed what to do
as I confront each mystery
that keeps from me the smallest clue,
forcing me to decide
to walk this way without a guide.

Thus I search the path alone,
chancing every step I take,
hoping that I won't stay prone
to dreams from which I won't awake,
and that from within my prayer
you'll lead this stumbler to your lair.

It seems that you are guiding me
through each muddle and each fall.
It's not your way of chiding me
but as a response to my call -
gently telling me that you
are groping through the acts I do.

I know the truth

I know the truth but walk it not.
Is there a greater hell than this?
When the only reality I've got
is divorced from its own bliss?

I know the solution is to decide
yet actually deciding not to do it,
not because my thoughts misguide
but my ignorance makes me eschew it.

I see the results of my stupidity
but inner sloth curbs my action
and prevents the rise of cupidity
that could bring me any satisfaction.

The hell is I choose not to rise
to where all my dilemmas vaporize.

The waiting

Unable to decide I wait.
The night is long and deep
while all I do is masticate
old dreams that haunt my sleep.

And in this dark I want to know:
"What is your will for me right now?
Show me the path that I should go.
I will take it. That's my vow."

But silence reigns though I heard
my own thoughts say: "Do anything!"
Why won't I trust this word
to avoid more pointless suffering?

Your answer to my prayer seems: "Act!
Then I can guide you on your way,
but to wait too long is to be sacked
by the very words you pray."

The closed door

I used to think I knew the way,
the reason-why that I am here,
that in all the words that I'd pray
I'd sense your presence loud and clear -
certain that you'd reveal to me
the essence of your mystery.

I was convinced that I was right.
You are! sufficient the reason to know
you would manifest in my night
to lead the path where I must go -
that you would never desert me
or permit life to truly hurt me.

But I was wrong for now I lie
in the bonds of a death so cruel
that even to think is to die,
and to know is to be a fool
who, with what he believes,
creates the way he self-deceives!

The open door I had is closed.
Our communion seems ended
so that my heart is now disposed
to a death that is suspended
in a state where I can see
but can't surmount my misery.

The end has come

The end has come and you have lost me . . .
My love is gone, forever over,
and it's as though life has tossed me
to where only vultures hover,
circling in the air above
the decomposition of my love.

I have squandered everything -
the peace and joy, the warmth and bliss,
with no ideas to which to cling
as I plunge into the dark abyss.
My love for you used to protect me
from my feelings that now reject me.

Indifferent and I do not care.
Diseased but I won't take the cure.
I find that I am suffering where
death is cruel and premature,
though I admit some blame is mine
but not willfully of my design.

I lost my drive and now I know
that I don't even want it back!
It's only downward that I go,
flung into the vacuum of my lack,
unwilling to avoid the crash
with the wall to which I dash!

My friends

They fled from me when I was crucified
and stayed afar when I gave up and died.
No one was with me at the very end
on whom my tears and sweat could depend.
They just withdrew and left me waiting where
a sepulcher was built from my despair.
Their distant smiles told me they had left
and like a miser I sat there all bereft
of the friendship for which I truly pined
but which they withheld when I was confined.
My peace came when I thought of Jesus Christ -
how he was abandoned when he was sacrificed,
and like his friends when he was resurrected
mine returned so that our love could be perfected.

Only you as I

When I stopped looking I saw;
ceased moving I arrived;
ended thinking I knew with awe
that my self had been revived.

In doing things I put spaces
where there never should be any,
then living in those false places
by making from the one the many.

In these fields I lost my way
and got caught in my own mind
where what I think, to my dismay,
are subtle chains that trap and bind.

Even you I put out there!
someone to whom I had to pray,
but I got lost in my own prayer
when I wanted my own sway.

Now I know that we are one.
All other claims are just a lie
and when these falsehoods are undone
what remains is you as I.

The grin of death

(After a night with heart problems)

Last night death looked at me and grinned
and I thought that my last moment had come.
It was not that I had fallen or sinned
but my heart syncopated like a toxic voodoo drum,
warning that the any moment I may sojourn
to the place from whence there is no return.

Yet there was no anxiety or fear in me.
Just a regret that I had not given more
and that I did not completely revere in me
the One who gave me the life that I adore.
I was ready to phase out from this place,
to shut the book and close the case.

Then I became aware of his mischievous smile.
Not that of someone seeking retribution -
who exacted revenge from me because of guile
or of a life that was lived in dissolution
but that of a friend I met many times before
who promised he would come later for an encore.

Hybernation

Where have my restrictions fled?
the restlessness in meditation?
sitting there in quiet dread
trying to develop moderation
while every muscle used to scream
in revolt against this regime?

Where is my habitual fury
that alienated every friend?
which my nature caused injury
with a smile meant to offend?
the anger which drove me where
angels fled in shocked despair?

Where is the lust that degrades
both the body and the soul?
that attacked with subtle shades
to make me lose my self-control?
the vice that was my heart's disgrace
and kept me fleeing from your face?

Where now the fear and pain that mauled
when tomorrow seemed like a vacuum?
The anxiety that so appalled
as I convulsed within its womb?
waiting for life to terminate
before it began to germinate!

I woke to find that here am I,
a free soul sitting in an open cage.
Now I can stretch my wings and fly
beyond the confines of my rage,
to freely roam the clouds above
in the expanses of your love.

In my sleep you cut the chains
that held me captive in my mind.
My world became so full of gains
the past, mere dreams I left behind -
dreams that you were mutilating
so I could stop my hibernating.

Deeply content

Deeply content I wait on you
to reveal the next step I must take
and to tell me what I must do
or what habits to forsake.

Great happiness pervades my soul
but it is not entirely complete
since I expect a different role
to make my rapture more replete.

Surely this can't be all there is.
Where is the beatific vision?
The real dialogue that prayer is
when knowing God's will with precision?

Yet I find in little things
your ever-new manifestation,
in each trivial act that brings
me to my knees in adoration.

Day by day you are expressed as I -
the I that's struggling on its way
until the moment that I die
and know that you were I at play.

Therefore I will wait till then
and live each instant with delight
and leave new roles to other men
who relish them with appetite.

You are my omnipotence

You are my own omnipotence,
yet I limit myself with prohibitions.
I cover my own innocence
with ignorance and divisions.
I obey the thoughts that sway
me to think there is no other way.
I rule myself with ideas that bar
so I can only move so far!

You are my omniscience as well,
but I insist that one can never know
and that only such formula can tell
the true path that I should go.
Yet in knowing you I know all things
and the expansion that it brings,
but still I subscribe boundaries to you
from my fractioned point of view.

You're everywhere and all I see,
but I stay satisfied with the veneer.
Since you are all the soul can ever be
how can I then give in to fear?
But I keep you from supporting me
when I'm struck by the enemy
who takes my thoughts, words and deeds
to conquer me as he misleads.

Thus I'm the lord of my own restriction:
I permit the darkness to come and rule me
and create, within, this absurd addiction
that is made to delude and to fool me.
But now that I understand I was mis-taught
and how I act upon these ideas I bought,
I can cast them away so I can be
the totality of the truth that breathes through me.

The jail

Again I walked into a jail,
except this one was rich and grand
and no one ever told a tale
of horror about this prison land.

Every inmate had his suite
where he was all too glad to dwell,
reclining on the plushest seat
as he was dining all too well.

I remember that with a key
I entered this unusual place
but I suppressed or would not see
that I was captive in its space.

I forgot that I could leave
until the dream scared me so
that I awoke then to perceive
the jail itself won't let me go.

A prison stays a prison still,
even if it's warm and good
when it deceives the human will
to live with what's not understood.

The noblest thought's a prison bar
unless our freedom stays intact!
for we can only move as far
as our beliefs pave the tract.

No matter how plush my jail
or poor my freedom seems to be
if I stay inside I will fail
to reach life's crowning victory:

Of being free inside my soul
where no thing can ever bind me
for when I break its control
I leave all jails behind me.

The power of the vow

The hardest thing I had to do
was to decide to change my ways,
to take the path direct to you
through sin's self-created maze.
And the only way that I could do it
was not to transgress or pursue it.

I had to vow my acts would cease
and in fear of you put on the brakes
so I could once more live in peace
away from sin's effects and aches.
I then found this vow released
great powers as my confidence increased.

I then turned to face the inner foe -
a fantasy, a mirage or a daydream
that only existed in what I know
or in delusion's dark extreme.
And with the power from the vow
I tamed the beast by living in the now.

Your will

To do your will, for nothing more I ask.
To love your will while I perform my task.
To know you are the doer of the act performed
and I the channel, by your grace transformed.

To share your will with everyone I meet
by showing through my acts your will replete
that those who fear your will brings only pain
may see in me they feared your will in vain.

The owl

The night rolled inwards like a fog
and shuts out all the images of day.
The wind chanted a weary monologue
to one and all within its way.
As I sat outside in the dark I heard
an owl sadly calling to its mate,
but in the wind the sound was blurred
so that its song would dissipate.
Yet in my heart an owl did hear
and quickly rose in answer to the call
and though the darkness did appear
to keep it caged inside its wall,
the owl within me knew what it should do
and slew the night to be with you.

I am spring

What music is it that I hear?
New rhythms bursting on my mind!
Melodies that haunt the ear
and leave all monotones behind.

What are the colors that I see?
Rainbows arching in the sky!
like flowers blooming endlessly,
dazzling as they gratify.

What the fragrances I smell?
incense, perfumes and life exploding?
that make me drunk as they impel
good attitudes that were eroding.

I feel the air awhirl around me,
bracing me with life and laughter,
telling me as they dumbfound me:
I am the spring that I am after.

Detachment

You create space for me to dwell in;
releasing me from any inner clinging
to people, ideas and things I fell in
and the hell that they were bringing.
You uncoupled me from attachment's glue
that bound me to outer forms and aims;
which not only controls me in all I do
but stake inside me their own claims.
But detachment provides me with liberty.
In it I can really live, love and prevail
and be whom I am truly meant to be -
even in those moments when I fall or fail
for you're God's grace that anoints me so
I'm free no matter what I do or where I go.

Faith

Faith gives me eyes to see
what's hidden from the intellect
and shows me things that cannot be
to the mind that must dissect.
It says that God is here and I believe
and thus I walk a hidden way
that will hoodwink and deceive
the understanding in its play.
For faith reveals and purifies
what the intellect will restrict.
Its dark brings light unto the eyes
the mind misleads and always tricked
but when the mind comes in surrender
faith brings it to its fullest splendor.

What Jesus taught

For years I struggled to define
the essence of what Jesus taught.
I sought in vain for its design
until my acts distilled his thought.

Christ came to serve and not to rule,
and that is how we all should be,
for only then are we his tool
to perfect human destiny.

He came to love and not to judge.
His law is that we love each other -
to forgive and hold no grudge
against a sister or a brother!

His example then is very plain:
to serve without wanting reward,
to give without a hope for gain
and to love all beings in the Lord.

It's when we rule and take, that we
create hate, envy and resentment,
but give and serve with charity
and we are sowers of contentment.

Our job is not to make a paradise
but to love and serve the Lord.
Then we'll find to our surprise
earth's paradise has been restored.

When he comes

When he comes
there are no drums
announcing his arrival
like trumpets blaring a revival!

Instead he manifests in quiet
when our thoughts have quelled their riot
and the soul, empty and still
is opened up for him to fill.

Then in silence he is revealed
from noises that keep him concealed,
'till all you see is made of him
whose presence fills you to the brim.

In quietness is strength and might.
In stillness arises wisdom's light.
From this calm and peace there flows
the love in which creation grows.

Beyond the noise, beyond the crowd
of minds and hearts that clamor loud
he waits for us to come and be
one in his silent ecstasy.

For solitude's his hiding place
and stillness reveals his unseen face
which all the time lurks in the heart
where noise and crowds keep him apart.

Assimilation

You assimilate my being into you,
absorbing my choice in your will,
and while I love you, as I gladly do,
it is your love that makes me thrill.
When I think of you it's you that I become!
My mind takes on your form and mood.
My own speech hearing you becomes so dumb
it flees my thoughts to speak only your good.
Your virtue now replaces my every vice.
Your joy casts out all my pain and gloom.
Your liberty for which there is no price
has set me free from bondage and its doom,
until you are all that now can remain
in this flesh that once was my domain.

The freedom of the eagles

When I behold the eagles fly
like masters of the endless blue,
I envy their place in the sky
where they are free to rendezvous,
but as I analyze I find
they're captive in a programmed mind.

I am much freer than they are!
I can fly where they can't go.
Though I be jailed behind a bar,
or caught in my fate's undertow,
I can glide and soar within
where no bird has ever been.

My inner sky has no confines -
above all instincts and their laws,
beyond duality's designs
that hide in life its fatal flaws,
and here's no form, no name or space . . .
Just joy and bliss and endless grace.

Eternal Spring

Through hardened snow the blossoms press
to burst upon the world their smiles,
lifting from our hearts the stress
that make us faint beneath our wiles.

Spring in winter's fiercest grip
that's how you break upon the mind
to call it into fellowship
so it would leave the cold behind.

The ice then melts and water runs
in bubbling streamlets down the slopes,
and light dawns like a thousand suns
to warm the heart with happy hopes.

Yet outside us winter still reigns
reminding us of its control
but where you bloom among our pains
eternal spring invades the soul!

To forgive

"Forgive," is what I hear you say.
"Then you'll be truly just like me
because there is no other way
for you to enter sanctity.

To excuse is to release
and let go of bitterness and hate.
Then your heart will bloom in peace
with the love you cultivate.

All pardon brings joy to your soul
from any rage you learn to quell.
So write this on your inner scroll:
'It's in your forgiveness that I dwell! ' "

Misspent

I thought my whole life was misspent;
that I had lived it all in vain.
I was so ease and pleasure bent
my actions could not bring me gain.
My years were lived to no avail
when ideas set me up to fail.

I milked the pleasure from my senses,
gratifying them, my urgent goal,
but in doing that I built fences
around both my heart and soul,
never guessing they kept out
the very joy I was about.

But now I feel they guided me
on the paths I had to go
or else they would have chided me
because of what I'd failed to know.
It came with clarity, at last,
I won't change any of my past.

In those exploits I now know
there was little else that I could do.
It's how life forced me to grow
by taking this zigzag way to you
since from each sin I have learned
that it was you that I had spurned.

And yet my wrongs were not all lost
since they did never satisfy,
and the emptiness that they cost
forced my fantasies to die;
to show my past was meant to be
the unraveling of this mystery.

How glad I am

How glad I am that youth is over.
I need no longer be a rover
that must taste and know all things.
It's not urgent to explore
where no one else had been before
so I can bathe in youth's eternal springs.

No longer do I need to know
why all the planets come and go
and what the past hid beneath the sand.
The why has given place to how
since time's restricted to the now
where life's unchartered and its course unplanned.

Facts no longer shape my fate.
Theories have ceased to fascinate
for wisdom comes when knowledge is applied.
Love reveals the truth within
while facts conceal their origin
and masks it with an overdose of pride.

Now my youthful drive is spent
my will is more resilient.
I need not master each thing big and small.
I need not conquer all I find
except the sly and restless mind
for to tame myself is to have conquered all.

A veil of lies

I am bled dry with well meant lies,
pious theories that claim they know
and high sounding promises that cauterize
the mind so that it cannot grow.

I have been hoodwinked by sincere folk
who claimed their doctrines were true,
while they placed on me their yoke
of holy denseness and its retinue.

I stand among the ruins of yesterday
asking the sky: where shall I live?
My foundations have all fallen away
and there's nothing left for me to give.

Slowly I break away from the past
into a life no one yet has explained
but at least it is a great contrast
of living in a mind that's faithfully profaned.

The time has come for me to realize
I'm the truth to which I so ardently aspire.
No one can give me what they hybridize
while only God can fulfill my desire.

As long as I am not completely free
I'm still a slave to ideas that are wrong
and no belief in any well worn mystery
can create the liberty where I belong.

The pain

The pain of the flesh I can bear
but that of the anguished soul
as it sweats from its despair
breaks down all my self-control
'till my life's bereft of meaning
as even God's not intervening.

Life plays tricks on the unsuspecting,
giving me all that I think I need,
not guessing that it is quietly directing
me to abandon all my lust and greed.
Except it does not give me light
to feel the mind and heart unite.

For as my dreams all disappear,
even though I have guts and hope,
life itself becomes so unclear
that I wonder how I can cope
as I leave the Eden of my dreams
for duality's brutal extremes.

Yet as I suffer I am forced to see
my pain as an anguished kind of work
that cleanses me from sense slavery
to the negative that I must shirk
because I've learned that in the end
this pain has been my ablest friend.

Plugged into you

Plugged into you there is perfection
where imperfections still abound.
My age-old manner of projection
no longer makes my pain profound.
Your power fills even my sleep
where dreams used to wail and weep.

I am free although my body's not.
Even so, its pain does not enjail
for when its shadow is my lot
despair and grief cannot prevail.
I can now see through their shape
as you become my great escape.

    For you are all and all in all,
    in the very moan I call
    and in surrender to your will
    the panacea for every ill.

    The sickbed becomes an alter where
    love's distilled from pure despair
    and for those who won't resist
    it is life's greatest alchemist.

Within our pain is your real presence.
Through its shape you've taken form
to distill in us the essence
of peace from our own inner norm,
for when we plug into your being
we stop at last all inner fleeing.

Total satisfaction

When you share your bliss with me
I'm meet because duality has passed
and confusion with its misery
are consigned to times that cannot last.

I'm consciously aware that we are one.
It's only you I now can perceive
and there is nothing different under the sun
that I am able to believe.

All is you when I am in your presence.
Everything glows and radiates.
Even weeds display an inner essence
that my soul authenticates.

Then what else is there for me to find?
to need? to seek? or to explain?
I am so pleased within my mind
I know there is no greater gain.

You are in me and I in you.
In you I think and feel and move,
and there's nothing left for me to do
or anything I have to prove.

When you are all I want

When you are all I want
I seek nothing more.
Your nature is to enchant
mine is to adore,
since in this worship I find
complete joy of every kind.

But when the tide flows
away from our intimacy,
and the association slows
down to a mere memory,
then I desperately seek outside
for places where you might hide.

Yet in my soul I know that you
cannot be absent if you tried.
Since you are I and it is true
such knowledge can't be denied.
But you can withhold your bliss
and I dread nothing more than this.

For you're my feeling you hold back,
my own response in adoration,
and my sufferings fill this lack
when I endure our separation,
since when you hide from me I'm not,
for you are all I am and got.

What I am

What I am is who you are in me,
that integral I that transcends
the flesh and its periphery
and the world on which it depends.

We're so one, division is an illusion
as you allow our thoughts to separate
and bring us under our own delusion
which acts as a legal opiate;

making it seem we're disconnected
to which idea we are so addicted
that our ignorance becomes perfected
and our awareness is restricted.

This oneness is not just a unity,
but sameness when adjuncts are deleted
and then we can claim with impunity
we're the gauge with which you are meted.

But this insane identification
with the flesh we claim as the 'I'
is the accepted abomination
that we all strive to justify.

Yet behind our sins and opposites
there is the I am that unites
but which the sluggish soul forfeits
with wrong ideas that it invites.

An overflow of love

When I overflow with love for you
I am dissolved in my adoration.
Then all I perceive is seen through
this love I am in exaltation.
Even thought pauses between us are filled
with the love that you over-spilled.

Then there is nothing I can need.
What else is there to satisfy?
when fear and pain cannot impede
the flow of joys that multiply,
since in you is every pleasure
and its fullness that I treasure.

As your love pervades each action,
there's fulfillment of all desire.
Just to think of you brings satisfaction
and the daily needs that I require.
Above all it makes me crave you so
you come to me in everything I know.

When I run away

When I run away from you
you follow me to lure me home
by giving me a point of view
that you engender through a poem.

They are the hounds of heaven
that pursue me as I go,
acting like a subtle leaven
so that I can always know

the path by which I should return
so I do not have to stray
and through their inspiration learn

I need not be a stow-away
in those assumptions that collide
with the truth that they defied.

Hidden music

I hear a music that haunts me
yet which I cannot sing aloud,
and its beauty ever taunts me
like a face behind a shroud.

It wakes me from the deepest sleep
to elude me and to make me ache
just to hear fractions while I weep
for missing it when I'm awake.

Yet when I go into sleep once more
to seek its melody and source,
it leads into my deepest core
as I follow its enchanting course,
where I find this polyphonic stream
creates the universe I dream.

The stillness binds

The stillness binds me to you.
Nay, simply brings you out in me
so that in everything I view
it is only you that I see.

Behind all noise silence reigns.
It is your throne upholding everything -
the humans, gods and their domains
wherever the saints and angels sing.

Out of your quiet comes all sound
and so they contain your impression.
Your silence is eternal all around
but sound is temporal transgression

so that we can turn to you and find
that you reveal yourself in stillness
once we have quieted the restless mind
of thoughts which are its only illness.

The dance of creation

You are the soundless sound
that hums around,
spinning your creation
and enjoying it through our sensation.

As a spider spins its web
you spin both our tide and ebb,
to catch the unsuspecting soul
into the limits of a role.

A puppet master pulls the strings
to which the dancer jumps and sings,
but the drama makes it clear
the puppet becomes the puppeteer.

Its dance brings freedom to the dancer
for behind it is the hidden prancer
who directs the drama with his skill
to absorb all players in his will

until the dance of creation
surges forth in great elation
of drawing back into its heart
the game that kept us all apart.

Solitude

My greatest joy is to be alone
and wallow in my solitude,
where silence expands to intone
swift glimpses of beatitude.

Stillness wraps me in surprise.
Each time it's different than before.
Its calmness makes me realize
it comes as your ambassador.

You then play hide and seek with me.
I find you where I least expect
as you evade my memory
to perplex my intellect.

Because I never can predict you.
Your thoughts are hidden from my ways
and my concepts can't restrict you
less self-love sets my heart ablaze.

Thus from the silence I expand
to embrace a peaceful plenitude
where I can come to understand
your dwelling place is solitude.

Everything reminds me of you

Everything reminds me of you.
It doesn't matter where I go,
what I think or say or do,
whether in sunshine, rain or snow
your loveliness keeps shining through.

You are the presence in each thing.
From your substance all is made
and the satisfaction that they bring
is only because your pervade
and are their basis and mainspring.

Through humankind you shine most clear.
In every person whom I see,
in their emotions, love and fear
you are the subtle mystery
that glows behind their thin veneer.

All life has you as its own base.
You project us into your creation
and behind each form your face
that we can see in contemplation
when yielding to your love and grace.

Why should I want to see you?

Why should I want to see you
when I would rather be you?
Think that we are far apart
when you dwell right in my heart?
Someone who is so close that I
know you are what I occupy?
The undying Self underlying me,
sustaining and sanctifying me?
So I can understand there is no you,
but Self from every point of view,
and what separates made to seem
fractured images that you dream!
Why should I look elsewhere
when I am in your only lair?

Even when I don't love you

Even when I don't love you I do.
Something inside me follows only you,
fretting that I do not even care
when I do not see you anywhere.
While I am surrounded with my pain,
caught in the web of an ugly mood,
unable to discern and see the good,
indifference smudges like a stain
and covers what is real in me with lies,
which the mind delights to believe,
caught in the patterns that deceive
until I rediscover my greatest prize:
the love that I crave at any cost
I have, to my amazement, never lost.

Your commandments inebriate

Your commandments inebriate.
Your laws are like the choicest wine
because their precepts liberate
the very heart that they enshrine.

Oh, how I hanker to totally obey
and observe these guidelines you have set.
Then I'll walk safely on my way
to live a life without regret.

Within your will lies our protection.
It guards against what evil is decreeing
and for those who fear not its correction
it creates within them your own being!

Now as I pray these words to you
my soul exalts in gratitude
because your will is what you do
to spread through us your magnitude.

The letter of the law

I suffocate beneath the letter of the law
that imprisons me with grief and pain,
when obedience demands that I abstain
being me and surrender to its rule of flaw.

I cannot help how heart and mind revolts
against the point of view which denies
what it reveres, but also crucifies
and with rigid dogma buries, lock and bolts.

No one should pour a person in a mold
and then say that this is God's will.
A law that frees must not be used to kill
unless it be the letter they uphold.

The laws that God made sets one free -
those of man forces one into a padded cell
where twisted reason stokes the flames of hell,
by stopping him from what he's meant to be.

Thus I decry the laws that such folk ossify
in tradition, ignoring change and growth,
choking spirit under banal rule and oath -
not knowing God to be the Self that they deny!

The chase

I thought that I was chasing you
when in reality it was my ideas of who
you really are that I was thus pursuing -
concepts causing all my misconstruing
behind which I would rush and hide
pretending that I had no pride.

I thought that I was loving you
in all the things that I would do -
like singing your praise to show you how
I lived and seriously took my vow,
but now I am shocked that I must see
that I was really only loving me!

Yet all is not lost in my urgent chase.
I find you all wrapped up in my case.
When not confusing body with the soul
you are the Self that I still extol
for when I seek and search and pry
you come to me as my exalted I.

Under attack

Just when I am content I sense
the enemy stalking in my mind,
not even hiding its pretence
of besieging me from behind.

It's as though I'm under fire
from directions that I don't expect
when everything that I admire
reveal to me their great defect.

All I can do is be amazed
when lovely objects so mislead
that all the ideas I had praised
made my happiness recede
because I forgot that things impart
their limitations to the heart.

I want to not want
(The battle)

I do not want to not want what I want
because my not wanting is too unsure
but when my memory begins to taunt
it makes not wanting seem premature,
and wanting is fueled by such desire
that not wanting is consumed in its ire.

Oh, I make sure my not wanting stays weak.
I turn my inner eye away so as not to know
that the fulfillment that I now seek
is a state that I never care to outgrow.
My not wanting is safely held in control
so that it can't be at the helm of my soul.

Yet there is this inner voice that says
that with my conflict I stay cleft in two
and that my tormented heart only strays
because I let it be tempted away from you
and as long as wanting and not wanting fights
I'm unable to exercise my spiritual rights.

But hard it is to make a lasting change.
The body has its own demands and tides
and the fantasy and memory can rearrange
facts and experiences, even a dream that hides
the truth behind its rationalizations and needs
so it never knows the lies on which it feeds.

Unyoking

I have let go of all self-discipline -
to be for once without restriction
that claims that I have to delve within
to relieve me of my inner friction.
I cast them off just to be truly free
from all the yokes imposed on me.

I have stopped laying those trips on me,
taking only those that life enforces.
Not what others claim that I should be
but what unfolds through my own resources.
I want to live without their imposition
that thus far brought me only division.

I'm now ceasing to have to and to must,
to ought to, to should and to try,
to abandon myself to and to trust
what others proclaim and testify.
I only want that which wells up in me
and solely as it does so spontaneously.

I rejoice I'm unyoked and unshackled,
surprised that I am still moral and good,
and the problems that I have tackled
have never been so well understood,
showing me that when I am truly free
there's nothing else but you that I can be.

How many dreams?

How many dreams before awaking?
phantasms that force us on and on!
Until we feel our hearts are breaking
and the dreams we cherish are all gone?
And what is left is just a glare
that spells no-thingness everywhere!

How much pain before we will see
that dreams are masters of delusion
and mothers of all our misery
as they deepen our confusion?
'till secret tears clear our sight
to see we live in a dream night?

Why won't we admit they're a decoy
that lead us from our inner peace,
yet from which we seek the joy
that only make our pain increase,
so that we won't believe that they
greatly mislead us on our way?

Why? I stormed until I find
we love to gorge on dreams that bring
on agony to maul the mind
with tons of futile suffering
because we fear but will not face
the One whom each dream must displace.

The catcher in the dream

Without you life is hell indeed.
No wonder we take to drugs and drink,
all to hide the glaring need
of you that drives us to the brink
of such despair and confusion
that we must escape its illusion.

We are trapped within your dream
in which there is a hidden catcher
who established in us his regime
before we face the great dispatcher
where the nightmare is so magnified
its agonies are doubly amplified.

But we're in love with the chains
the catcher locks onto our wrists,
and we gladly suffer all his pains
from the drunken dream that insists
this world is all that really is:
a mix of dreams with lots of fizz.

The only cure is to stop dreaming,
to wake and see that there's a way,
and that the dreams we're so esteeming
is how the catcher holds his sway,
and unless we break from his control
he remains the butcher of the soul.

Fire child   (a dream)

Suddenly my world was burning -
flames leaping up from everything!
fire lapping, reaching, churning
in wild, ecstatic shuddering,
but instead of being doomed
the outer world burnt ever free
for what I saw was not consumed
by the great heat and energy.

The incandescent hills were glowing
while clouds were shimmering with light,
with molten rivers wildly flowing
like gleaming serpents in the night.
And everywhere the fire clinging
outrageously to every shape,
while the atoms all were singing
and thriving in the firescape.

As red blue flames licked at my skin,
no burns or blisters would arise,
but when they entered my within
the fire darted from my eyes,
cov'ring and penetrating deep
as they transformed to revive
and wake matter from its sleep
to be for once truly alive.

Then I danced on the flames of gold,
and breathed them deep into my lungs
for their warmth made me bold
as they caressed with flickering tongues.
And as I whirled within the fire
breaking loose from form and frame
my soul was reaching ever higher
until I knew I am the flame.

The senses

The senses are the enemy
with the desires they engender,
creating within us a gluttony
of which mind is the prime offender
until one starts to behave
like a dulled, will-broken slave.

They are the lords of every pleasure,
not caring that they bring on pain
and the sensations that they treasure
are emissaries of death's domain
where everything is the reverse
of that which rules the universe.

They are our freedom and our jail.
Uncontrolled they flog the soul
and sap the will so it must fail
to spawn the light of self-control
without which we must endure
our life as a caricature.

But disciplined they point the way
to which we secretly aspire
and will not lead us astray
when we have conquered their desire
for then we come to understand
the flesh we wear is holy land.

The Buddha told me

The Buddha told me: "Take the road
that leads between the two extremes.
Neither to sorrow sing your ode
or seek pleasure from your dreams.

I can only point the way
but you must walk it on your own
for the strength with which to slay
delusion comes from you alone.

You will glimpse in solitude
and silence what you really are
for it is with your attitude
that you may push the door ajar

to see what only you can see
when you arise above those dreams
that keep you trapped to the degree
that you concede to their extremes."

Self-deception

It's the ego that creates division
by wanting to be the only cause
and in doing that creates derision
that stimulates its fears and flaws.
This sense that I'm better than another,
even though I know it's not the case,
and I am willing to degrade my brother
to bring him lower than my base
is the real Satan that dwells within,
where we won't go or dare to seek
since under the barriers of our sin
we're forced to see that we are weak
and where we find what we believe
is how we're forced to self-deceive.

We buy into lies

We buy into other people's lies because
we cannot find the real truth on our own
since it's hard to detect subtle laws
even with an aptitude full grown.

We also believe in their unproven tales
because our lethargy and laziness
prevent us from tearing down the veils
that reinforce our timeless craziness.

We want truth handed to us on a platter,
all nicely and neatly spelled out
so that it will console and always flatter
especially when we take a faulty route,
but if we don't search and stay misled
we might as well admit that we are dead.

A gift of love

Sometimes without any provocation
love sets my arid heart aflame,
with my soul as the oblation
that only you, my Lord, can claim.
A gift unsought, humbly received.
How generous you are to me,
for never would I have believed
it blossomed so gratuitously . . .
to show me that it comes from you!
Not something that I could have earned.
Not the results of what I do
or my affections now returned,
but simply love for its own sake
in which my love now can partake.

You come to me

You come to me in many ways!
Sometimes as love within my chest;
ofttimes lounging in my praise,
responding as the Inner Guest.

You frequently come disguised
as persons for whom I do not care
and I am shocked and so surprised
to see when you're emerging there.

I find you easily in health,
in happiness or in a friend.
You're sparkling in obvious wealth
or in any good that I attend.

You also come as pain and dread
to share your suffering with me.
It's hard to see you there instead
of the cruel and blatant agony.

You appear in all conditions,
teaching how I should adjust
when making new transitions
should I waver in my trust.

But in these 'comings' I have seen
it's not an entrance that you make
since you have always been
one with the life that I partake.

You seem hidden 'till I conceive
what I really see out there
is not what I crave to believe
but your Self to which I'm heir.

And that can only be when I
realize that I am one with you.
Then what I see can testify
that you are all I ever knew.

I sought you

I sought you in all things sublime,
sure that you'd be shining there,
instead I found you every time
in things for which I didn't care!
I sought you in drills of the mind
where intellects reveal and reign
but found you when I became blind
to the glories that they feign.
Their excellences only say
that whom you seek went 'that-a-way!'
whereas blindness to things declare
that you're encountered everywhere -
when forms and attributes are transcended
then you, at last, are apprehended.

A moment of glory

Your presence burns within my soul
and enflames me with such pleasure
that tears spill out of all control
for having within me this treasure.
Your presence, yes, this glorious I
contents, fulfills and delights me so
it is the very essence of the why
I live and whom I care to know.
You glow and I share your rapture
from the secret places of my being,
because it seems that you now capture
everything that I am seeing
until all is I and I is surely you
and what I feel is how I know you do.

How vast you are!

How infinitely vast you are!
So great you embrace all that is!
What I see as a little star
could be lights of distant galaxies.
I ask myself: "How can this be?
How can he who embodies everything
be intimately concerned with me
who's but a minor underling?"
But now I know the reason why
you had to come as a human being,
so we can understand and identify
with the form that we are seeing -
astonished at the glorious phenomenon
that you're indwelling every one!

The body

The body fights its inner battle -
desires that rise and lusts that rattle
and my whole flesh runs the tide
of reaching for the world outside.
And while any mood is in sway
it only wants its own way,
revolting against the discipline
when it pines to plunge in sin.
But when I break down its will,
suddenly all's calm and still -
a temple where I love to dwell
and yearning cannot cast its spell,
a place so charming and diverse
as to contain the universe!

New laughter

Again there is laughter in the wind.
The dark is full of smiles and cheer.
In places where my fear has sinned
now only goodness can appear.
The night exudes a hidden light
as low clouds churn a holy rain
that wipes all sadness from my sight
and makes a gladness of my pain.
Hell's memory has fled from me -
left an experience of learning
which aim it is to set me free
from the body's endless burning.
And the glare that blinded me?
Your light through which I couldn't see.

You can be met with

You can be met with in the now -
not in the future or the past.
It's in the present you endow
the heart to move into the vast
where it can escape its jail
of dreams that are its great travail.

In the quiet mind you are reflected
when thoughts and feelings disappear,
and vision becomes so perfected
your very mysteries seem clear,
for all things then reveal how you
are present in the acts I do.

Retreating from the world's allure
you hide behind whate'er I see
'till my love for you is so secure
that you are all that I can be,
not as the God who rules the earth!
but as a child who shares his worth.

Desert silence

In the quietness I hear
silent footsteps coming near.
With the hush of my inaction
comes the perfect satisfaction
of sensing you in this frontier.

Since no problem now surrounds me
and no earthly worry hounds me
something opens in my mind
and I feel myself unwind
'till only peace abounds me.

Though I know that you are here
I still can't coax you to appear.
The space between us seems too fixed
and our textures so unmixed
that our difference is forever clear.

Yet suddenly the hidden screen
that has forever come between
you and me at last being to rend
bursting open 'till in the very end
no difference between us can be seen.

The world of silence

The world of silence is your robe
and solitude the way you probe
deep into the heart to teach
where noisy words can never reach.

He who cannot be alone
lives the life of a stone
which of itself can't move
outside the prison of its groove.

But he who turns away to be
alone with you in privacy
finds in seclusion you impart
all knowledge to the hungry heart.

I love once more

And so, at last, I love once more,
or did my action ever cease?
because I find within my core
a vast expanse of living peace.
When my joy and love submerged
I felt bereft of any hope
but now I sense my will was purged
and given strength with which to cope.
I see now that you have the power
to give or take, to curse or bless,
because my joy can only flower
when you bestow your happiness
and all the pain, to my surprise,
was really loving in disguise.

You are the love I feel

You are the love I feel right now.
It is your presence pervading me
with the power that won't allow
myself to be degrading me
for this response does reveal
that you are this love I feel
otherwise you won't appear
and manifest your presence here.

This love is wholeness and elation,
meant to make me realize
that out of my contamination
can arise the greatest prize:
the Sole Being that makes me see
I am my friend or enemy
and to judge myself is to scorn
the one in whom I am reborn.

Understanding

From the awareness of our unity
flows a chaste divinity.
This sweetness that I entertain,
enjoy but never can explain
is truly whom you are in me.

When we are thus fused as one,
our joy vibrates in unison.
I feel so complete and whole
delusion can't confuse my soul
and pain left for oblivion.

But withdraw this blisss from me
and little seems as it should be.
Again I feel that we are two
and there is nothing I can do
except implore your company.

One day this see-saw will abstain
to bring me both pleasure and pain.
My inner patterns will lose force
to veer me further off my course
and only whom you are will then remain.

A worn out role

Mountains look like silhouettes that delude me;
trees like props in a studio of a movie show.
I feel that this life does not include me
and bars my way so that I can't perceive or know.
It seems that I freely submit to co-operate
because I cannot conceive of anything better
and thus I am self-forced to perpetuate
the dream I know to be a lie to the letter.
Anything appears to be finer than the unknown
where I may find something that I can't control,
and thus I can't help choosing to walk on alone
acting with mechanical fervor in a worn out role
where it's better to be safe in a stale disguise
than healthy and free in a life I improvise.

The stone

The sun and wind and rain
take their revenge on me
since I've been on this terrain
for an eternity.
My own inertia holds me still
and pulls me down into the earth,
robbing me of any will
to press on for a greater worth.
People sometimes come and take me
to toss about or build a wall
but one thing will not forsake me:
the very ground on which I fall,
which gives me a place to lie
while I contemplate the sky.

A veiled romance

You are living right inside me
but I can't pinpoint the place.
Yet I can feel your ecstasy
filling me with love and grace,
setting my being all afire
with the love that you inspire.

Suddenly my heart starts singing
songs I've never heard before
and these kindnesses are bringing
you across from rule and law
into my heart so it can dance
with you in a veiled romance.

Now my very joy betrays you,
telling me that you are here,
and whatever cause delays you
need not ever make me fear
for you're so close I cannot see
you've always been living through me!

I live by faith

I live by faith and now I know
without it I am truly lost
since it outlines where I must go
so that I pay no bitter cost.
It is my own responsibility
which I acknowledge and confess
to guard my own tranquillity
from corruption and distress.
I must practice what you say,
even if it seems that I will die,
because you are the only way
that I have to prove or try,
trusting that at last I'll see
with faith you weave life's tapestry.

The fall

There is a raging inside me,
an anger against the tyranny,
the subtle way in which I'm jailed
with attitudes I tried and failed,
and left me stranded in the mesh
that I have spun from my own flesh!

Some say it's karma that I earned
from lessons that I never learned.
But who made the law that corrects
flaws no unwitting heart suspects?
yet has to pay with great devotion
since he set that law in motion?

Others state I've the will to choose
and for that I must pay my dues,
but where's the wisdom that should go
with this free will that it can show
in justice what path I must take
to lead me from its pain and ache?

Out of your Self you made
the universe and its charade.
You became its living creatures
with its variety and features,
giving you the right to play
the game you made in your own way.

Thus I must suffer and endure,
hoping that I always can be sure
that at the end of this long wait
I can have no greater fate
than being one with him who's the real me
for my own identity.

Now in my umbrage I can see
that it is God groping through me,
and also that I should bless
all failure as steps to success
instead of censuring your laws
that make me suffer from my flaws.

It's you who set up this show,
you who walk the paths we go.
You who suffer every fate
that your laws can create,
and yours the right to make the rules
to educate these grumbling fools.

Hence everything is in its place,
resting securely in your grace.
The only defect is our choice
as it disregards your voice,
projecting from our wills the curse
of an imperfect universe.

You welcome me

You welcome me as I come home,
and draw me in your sweet embrace
so that I lose the urge to roam
as you become my sacred place.

Your love holds no recriminations.
You smile and all is right for me.
You wipe out my abominations
as you become a light for me.

In your love my guilt disappears
for your forgiveness makes me whole
as you erase all my pain and fears
and you govern within my soul.

The past is gone and there's only now.
It's in this now time that you reign
and from where you lavishly endow
a love that cannot wax or wane.

Crossroads

When nothing outside satisfies
I walk on in a no-man's zone,
among the rubble that comprise
the things to which I was prone.

I see them now as from afar,
like a mirage on the sand,
and like my life a bit bizarre,
it cannot wet or cool the land.

The outside does not mean a thing,
except to delude and enjail,
where success can only bring
the bitter feeling that I fail.

To look outside for the goal
is to battle with that which dies,
and then to subject my soul
only to things that penalize.

So here I stand on the crossroads
and cannot choose a way to go.
I do not have the drive that goads
me to the state where I can know.

It makes my darkness darker still.
I don't know how to enter where
I'll find that which must fulfill
as the mystics all forswear.

But choose I will and choose I must
or I will just wait here and turn
until I'm screwed into the dust
and I am doomed to never learn.

Behind the emptiness I feel

Behind the emptiness I feel
there is a fullness waiting to be known,
a force that can renew and heal
and no one ever can disown.

But there is a veil that blocks
the mind from entering the heart
and which the will at last unlocks
so mind and heart can't tear apart.

Unseen and not discerned by the senses
it's just an idea that holds it there,
not sins but mental influences
that keeps the soul so unaware
that it comes as a shock to see:
I am that fullness that I keep from me.

When I plan

What you give me I will take.
No more shall I plan to make
my foolish dreams come true
since they lead away from you.
Let your will for me unfold.
I will flow along its stream
until, at last, I shall behold
you are revealed in every dream!
Thus I shall search no more
so you can manifest in me.
In each moment I'll adore
you as my own identity
so I can see that when I plan
I remain just a worldly man.

Stages

As I review my life I see
it's all a game that we play,
but the rules we think we know
keep changing day by day
until we're forced to stand and shout:
"I don't know what life is all about!"

It seemed like a carousel
when I was just a boy,
on which I rode 'till I was drunk
and hungover with joy.
I sowed my oats with fun and glee
and reaped myself its misery.

Life became a circus next
where each one clowned a role.
Believing all the silly games
we lose our self-control
because we can't accept that we
are better than our repartee.

It looked like an asylum
as I grew on in years,
with people frozen in their roles
and crippled with their fears.
It seemed perverted and so strange
to know they'd rather die than change!

As I wizened I realized
life is a slaughter house,
where circumstances toy with us
as cats do with a mouse,
except that in this lion's den
men were consuming other men.

Life is what it is, and that
is what I finally saw.
Not to interpret or expect,
to seek or ask for more.
Just to take what it would give
became the prudent way to live.

Since I surrendered to its flow
life has set me free.
Now that I've unmasked its truth
how can it threaten me?
I see since freedom made me whole
it's God parading as each soul.

You come as dusk

You come as dusk to force our minds
to enter quietly in prayer
and withdraw from all that binds
our hearts to its worldly care.

We close our eyes as not to see
temptations knocking at our senses,
as darkness shades with mystery
and sets up our own defenses.

For in the darkness we can meet
him who made us for his pleasure
and who in silences discreet
reveals to us his hidden treasure.

The day, you said, is made for man
but night for God and concentration
that in the dark each of us can
meet you in our meditation.

The kiss divine

Whom you have kissed, my own,
no one else may dare to kiss
for it is you and you alone
who can bestow eternal bliss.
Our fleshly joys are counterfeit,
no matter how pleasant and sweet.

But the kiss of love you give
ends every kind of suffering.
Its rapture grants the urge to live
and flower into unending spring,
while the love your touch supplies
is the drive that sanctifies.

Oh! madness of that kiss divine
brings such sweetness to my soul
that heaven floods this heart of mine
'till joy becomes my only role
since where your bliss once came as guest
is hallowed ground, forever blessed.

Within my heart

Within my heart I feel your calm,
showing me I'm in the right place.
Even the flesh becomes a balm
when permeated with your grace.
Into the emptiness I felt before
came your presence bringing peace
that welled from deep within my core
to give my life a joyful lease.
How warm and safe our oneness feels
where no fear can enter to distract,
and no matter what pain fate deals
in loving you the negative is lacked,
for as long as you remain with me
I cannot find a single enemy.

The leash of my senses

(After over-eating at a wedding.)

I'm led by the leash of my senses,
like a bull with a ring through the nose,
and in spite of my foolish pretenses
I go where the sense leash goes.

A little bell rings and I drool.
A red flag flaps and I charge.
My instincts make me react like a fool
and behave like a mad man at large.

It's not that I don't have control
but just that I don't want to use it,
and I'll manipulate every loophole
so I can remain as I am and excuse it.

Thus with my choice I shape my fate,
not knowing the dream in which I dwell
might just well be that lamentable state
that the scriptures declare to be hell.

Dream Identity

In a dream without stop
I climb a mountain steep and high,
and though it seems I see the top
the summit e'er denies my eye
the pleasure of seeing it there.
As I plod onto the next plateau
I always find to my despair
there still are endless tiers to go.

In looking back the views inspire
me to climb on through each cloud
into a new and endless higher
where stillness reigns fierce and loud
and I discover that all I see
is but a dream reality.

Between extremes

There is no middle way for me.
I am torn between the two extremes.
Either I'm conscious of eternity
or sucked in the whirl of dreams.

When I am awake I am the master
of my senses and the world around me
but in dreams I weave disaster
from the problems that surround me.

Either I famine or I feast.
I sin with a fury that disgusts me,
or else I behave like a holy priest
where everyone loves and trusts me.

It's on this razor's edge that I was born,
on the frontiers of genius and insanity
where I find I either love or scorn
the exploration of my own humanity.

The pot of gold

When I get what I want I find it was a lie.
There is no satisfaction in obtaining things,
and no matter what I gain it does not satisfy
but leaves me empty with greater hankerings.

When I look to the without for my contentment
I feel betrayed when life does not produce it
and I sense a hidden but deserved resentment
when I am forced to justify or to excuse it.

It's a mirage in a dream that I am chasing,
pots of gold where rainbows don't even exist,
fantasies where goals for me are so debasing

that when I achieve I feel like I have missed,
but what I resent most is not having been told
to look inside me is to find the pot of gold.

Jolt

The greatest jolt I ever have received
was to know that I know nothing, now or then,
and that all my knowledge only deceived
and that which I now know may delude again.
For that which I thought I had achieved
were only fantasies in which I had believed,
on which I based my life and attitudes
but now seem only sugar-coated platitudes -
a pacifier onto which I held and sucked,
thinking that I was truly nurtered and fed,
a placebo life gave and then viciously plucked
and now gives me nothing to use in its stead,
except that I am nothing and what I know
is a misleading dream that isn't really so!

If only . . .

Standing before your picture I heard you say:
'You can get out of this if you so choose,'
and I knew I could but unwisely chose to stay
in the state where I was doomed to lose.

And now I find myself trapped by this decision.
I came to the fork and took the easy route
that led me in the end to this arid prison
that is the bequest of the indolent devout.

I feel like a man mutilated and castrated,
who yearns to lay a maiden the whole long night,
yet knowing it's but a dream he's cultivated
to live off his powers like a leech or parasite.

Now I can only cry in cliches about my pain.
If only I had analyzed your words with care!
If only . . . if only I could go back once again
I'd chose the route the senses all foreswear.

My peace has come

My peace has come as a pure gift.
I knew I could not escape the snare
since my fall was sure and swift
and I was splattered everywhere.

I tried to find an escape route
where I could put some plans in action
but my sins claimed such a clout
and would permit me no retraction.

I knew that I was firmly bound,
waiting for my tapes to be erased,
suffering the threats they expound
and smothered in what they encased.

But when I woke I was surprised.
Gone the chains of thoughts and feelings;
gone the sloth that penalized
me in all my acts and dealings.

You gave freedom where there was none
so that here I stand once more
with every foolishness undone
as joy and bliss reign evermore.

I can only wonder in surprise,
mouth agape and intellect defeated
for the one who was so self-penalized
has now a heart with joy repleted.

The Master

I never found you, Master,
in the words that I would pray.
No matter what I said
you always seemed so far away
until I found that words can hide
the truth behind their subtle pride.

The best prayers I now pray
is when I have nothing to say.
I wait and my heart swells
to where God in his glory dwells
but more is said and more is heard
than if we used up every word.

I never found you, Master,
though I looked in every place.
I crossed the land and ocean
always looking for your face
until I found it's not outside
but in the heart where you abide.

It's you I now behold
in every person, rock and tree.
No matter what I look at
you are looking back at me!
and now I have found to my surprise
that you are looking through my eyes!

The grinding

Grind me down, Lord, grind me low.
Grind me as deep as I must go
to break through onto your plane
where I can rise above all pain
to know, at last, that as you grind,
you grind attachment from my mind.

What I cling to mother's pain.
What I don't give up diseases me,
and what I hold onto in vain
in the end displeases me,
for what was sweet now turns sour
as life unplugs it from your power.

Strip me then of all desire,
of attachments that incarcerate,
for the very things I now admire
in the end I'll learn to hate.
They promise all but can't deliver -
a taker masking as a giver.

Pain and grief cannot degrade
a soul that learned how not to cling
for only that which I have made
can cause my pointless suffering,
because as all my desires cease
your freedom blossoms in my peace.

Let me die

Let me die before I die
then there will be no death for me -
only a passage from the lower I
into my own identity -
for death's a trap to encage
the battered soul with its own rage.

A jail that enslaves the mind
with the idea that hypnotizes,
so as the years go by we find
this lie cheats and paralyzes
us into thinking we are mortal
on this side of death's portal.

There's only life within the soul
that no one can take away,
and death has a confined role
to prod the heart to search and pray
so it can find the Lord within,
beneath the rubble of its sin.

But our ideas are hard to slay
and all their lies become so true
that they lead the mind astray
with the dreams they will pursue
till in the end we can't believe
they torture us without reprieve.

Without relevance

Without relevance my will collapses
as my energies scatter without direction,
like pus that is squeezed from an abscess
and spills everywhere its foul infection.

Lacking dreams my mind destroys its vision,
leaving me stranded in self-derision.
while the energy that once defended
now attacks what it once befriended.

And I feel that I'm self-devoured
as flesh and spirit battle for my soul,
that can never assume a stable role
when its will to live is deflowered.
All that then remains is the pain
that keeps my vision split in twain.

The failed system

What I believed and what I'm now
are as day and night, with day as night
so that I can't understand how
night robbed day of its own light!
I'm stripped bare without protection -
walking in a world that doesn't care,
and all I feel is a rude rejection
which has become my daily fare.
The old self is transformed and I
am a stranger I cannot recognize,
nor can I begin to fathom why
I seem that which reality belies.
The old system has failed me so
I never dreamed I did not know.

Pain, the uninvited

You came unsought to stay with me
and lodged yourself within my hip,
circling yourself with misery
as you tightened your own grip
so that I can only move and do
on the course outlined by you.

Unceasingly you gnaw at my bones,
while the flesh tenses up in pain
and I can hear my muffled groans
and the wretchedness they contain,
for you so control my concentration
my mind collapses in vexation.

You command my every action,
my thinking process and my sleep,
giving you the cruel satisfaction
of hearing how I cringe and weep,
and how I grind my teeth to still
the ceaseless pain that racks my will.

You've come to show me how to bear
that which I never felt before,
and how I always ought to wear
the body around my inner core.
I took for granted that I could withstand
each problem that life would demand.

But now I am reduced to your effect,
for only you decide what I can do.
My independence is so wrecked
that I take all my clues from you -
who came to teach me I must be free
even when you strike and torture me!

Curtain time

Bring down the curtain aft' the play.
Turn off the lights and lock the door.
There's no place here for us to stay -
just vacant seats on a cold floor.

There are only ghosts on the dark stage,
the memories of a haunted past,
of loves and wars ideas would wage,
of schemes well laid that didn't last.

It seemed so real, the roles we played.
Dishing out what we were taught to crave,
but then at curtain time we were betrayed
with corpses tossed into the grave.

For life's a rack on which we're bound,
a nightmare drama we will not forsake,
but when the curtain falls it is found
our precious roles were all a fake.

My insanity

My insanity is knowing what is right,
understanding what choice should be made
yet doing only that which brings delight
even though its pleasures punish and degrade.
It is consciously putting on the chains,
locking them and throwing away the keys
and then trying to alleviate the pains
that exacerbate into a chronic disease.
It is a knowing that one can escape
but doing nothing to bring it all about
and willingly accepting the daily rape
without objecting with a single shout.
It's my chosen state that invites and clings
to ceaseless, self-engenered sufferings.

Imprisoned

I can't see out of my own jail.
Only I stare back at me,
to show me that what makes me ail
is my own aimless energy.

Each bar is a rigid thought,
solid idea that shuts me in
but which I freely bought
to shape my own discipline.

And what I project outside
onto the world I yearn to see
are the lies that hide
its veracity from me.

Break out! But how? I cry in vain
How can I be what I am not?
How can I make it rain
when I can't even stop my rot?

I try to control my mind
but failure brings me to despair
for the light that burned me blind
is one that wasn't ever there!

Fooled by surfaces

Fooled by surfaces and bound by lies,
by the pairs of opposites misled,
we receive distortion for our prize
while the truth we seek remains unsaid.
We can't interpret our perceptions,
but we cling to its glittering stimulation.
That is the pinnacle of our damnation
when we can't see through their deceptions.
And then we stand in shock or wonder
when the veneer of things forsake us
and grumble as we trudge along under
dreams constructed solely to break us
so that we always remain their effect
as their role is to trick and to reject.

In the rain last night

Walked down by the sea
in the rain last night.
My heart beat restlessly
in the rain last night.
A foghorn was blowing
in the rain last night.
It's lonely sound was growing
in the rain last night.
Rising and falling,
warning and calling
but no one answered
in the fog and the rain,
in the rain.

Had a frightened dream
in the rain last night.
Still can hear my scream
in the rain last night.
The waves stormed straight at me
in the rain last night
and flung me viciously
in the rain last night.
Roaring and rushing,
crowding and crushing,
Tossing me from wave to wave
in the rain.

A ship wrecked out at sea
in the rain last night.
Seemed like it was me
in the rain last night.
Didn't hear the horn
in the rain last night
and so it couldn't warn
in the rain last night,
but how can you hear
through waves of your fear
when passion fling you
on the rocks of your pain
in the rain?

I listen for you to speak

I listen for you to speak
in the silence where I wait on you,
with a heart and mind that seek
and hope that they can relate to you;
that you will open up my eyes
so that they can specialize
in what will make me resonate to you.

My ears hear the stillness ring
like a gong that's struck inside
and the silences that bring
to every thought an eventide.
There are no words but a flow
that tells me more than I can know
of my own soul where you abide.

In this wordless dialogue I unfold,
opening up to you like a flower
that drinks the rays of morning gold
or is revived in a springtime shower
until I am so caught up in your being
and the wholeness its decreeing
I've joyously surrendered to its power.

Finding you

When you manifest in me
I am satisfied and content.
I need nothing externally
to increase my betterment.

What else is there to desire?
The things I lack come of their own.
There are no cravings to expire
when all's contained in you alone.

And when you're overflowing me,
spilling lavishly the bliss you bring,
I rejoice in my delightful destiny:
In finding you I have found everything!

A hollow tube

A hollow tube without plaque -
that is what I crave to be,
so that in my total lack
you alone are all to me.
Without obstructions in the way
for space that you should occupy
just emptiness you can inveigh
with an eternal, newer I.
Fill all of me, for that I yearn.
Fill the self I crave to be
for in this dying I discern
that you always have been me,
hiding in the shadow play
of the self that I portray.

Obedience

To obey is the routine
that our faith must pursue.
Then what was unseen
will be made visible by You.
For obedience is the way
by which we are merged
and leads us when we stray
to Itself where we are purged.
It is the path that we must go.
It is the truth that we must know,
the very life that we can live
as we struggle to forgive,
but most of all it unveils the Christ
in which all selfishness is sacrificed.

The right decision

In stillness I am regenerated.
My center is pierced with delight
for all my sins are exonerated
when their guilt has taken flight.

You come only by my invitation
and will not force yourself on me
for it is in my quiet contemplation
that you come to set me free.

And when my surrender is complete
I am so absorbed in your presence
even memories of pain are obsolete
and destroyed by your incandescence.

Then there is nothing else but you
and in this completion I am filled
with your consciousness in all I do
until I am all you ever willed.

The prodigal

Here I am, Lord. I've come back
full of laughter, joy and cheer,
walking safely on the track
because I know that you are here.

I sense your presence in my heart.
There's no space for another feeling.
My negatives had to depart
for your closeness set them reeling.

Your love bursts from my every pore.
I sing and dance and shout within
where whom I had been waiting for
now took the place of my own sin.

All that remains is that which Is.
The ego fled without a cry
to make way for the Greater Bliss
that only you can occupy.

Dream counsel

Last night my dreams showed me my blunder:
My life lacks purpose and an obvious goal.
Without these I am bleakly trudging under
the burden of a false or poorly defined role.

I woke up crying out in a touching song:
Give me a purpose for my goalless existence,
a living function so that I can belong
and strive ahead with more persistence.

Then I saw that it is my lack of desire
that emasculated me without my knowing,
that robbed me of my energy and fire
and derailed me from where I was going.
I then knew I must slay all ambition
but work as those who make it a tradition.

When I read your words

When I read your words I burst aflame
for they're living sparks of spirit
and from their fire I can soundly claim
knowledge of God and how he can confer it.

Your consciousness then permeates my soul
as with their power gently inspiring me;
instilling in me a grand and newer role
while with a splendid love attiring me.

They materialize you right inside my heart.
Such sweetness pierces me that I can swoon
for then I sense how you fill each part
of my inner soul and mind as we commune -
to show me they come from the very source
that guides all creation on its course.

Out of nothing

God, I am empty and so void
it seems my very heart's destroyed,
yet as I live in this vacuum
I sense there is endless room
for your presence to be enjoyed.

The veil between you and my soul
is made of self-will and its role -
the acts of merely living
for fun and not for giving
but with pleasure as its goal.

But in this emptiness I find
more than simply peace of mind.
In its openness you enter
to become my only center,
ignoring everything I left behind.

I must be an empty shell
in which you can freely dwell,
for in the choice you gave
I dig or vacate the grave
that clogs your flow into my well.

Yet it's from nothing that you made
the universe that you pervade.
Now from my emptiness you must
recreate me from my dust
'till what I am is how you are conveyed.

Whom you are

My thoughts of whom you are
stand between you and me.
It is these concepts that mar
what human eyes can never see.
My sad efforts to define you
are why I'm doomed to malign you.

But you are beyond the mind,
even behind the human soul,
but the facts that keep us blind
are wanting to be in control,
submitting you to our logic
as our puffed up ego's frolic.

You hide behind our intellects,
far from every vain desire,
beyond what the heart projects
and to what our dreams aspire . . .
Beyond the senses and their play
in a beyond-thought hide-a-way

that's everywhere uncircumscribed!
The being who sustains the game,
who cannot be bought or bribed,
whose love shines on all the same
and who can only be discerned
once the mind has been adjourned.

When my heart and mind run dry

When my heart and mind run dry
and my will's devoid of force
I just want to let go and die
severed from my inner source,
and cut off from the world without
things cannot grow or even sprout.

Then I merely drift along,
placed here and there by circumstance,
that like a long, hypnotic song
lulls my soul into a trance
where what I find then deceives
like fantasies a day-dream weaves.

All light is withdrawn from me
because I lost this inner power
and robbed of my own liberty
an ennui rises to devour
the well from which there springs
the waters of which my joy sings.

But I have learnt not to resist.
I drift on with life's subtle tides
until I leave the chilly mist
behind which my pole star hides -
and realize that I had gained
much more than if only happiness had reigned.

No more

Fighting all my thoughts are worse
than fighting hordes of Saracen.
At least they die or disperse
but my thoughts resurrect again
as they venture to profane
my spirit on its own terrain.

It is in my mind that I battle,
where I fight myself viciously
and my forces shake and rattle
when ideas strike maliciously -
forcing me to live and obey
precepts that always lead astray.

No more, O God! No more! I cry
Enough of forcing down my urges
which I can only mollify
when my imagination splurges
but leaves me so wrenched in two
I feel outraged and torn from you.

No more all this inner lynching!
this endless self-depreciation!
that sends me wretching, squirming, flinching
in persisting self-alienation
just because I cannot be
what I surmise you want from me!

The bridge

I can't bring myself to cross the bridge
that spans the abyss between you and me.
I know it is a blatant kind of sacrilege
to sit in jail when I could walk out free.

I even know the bridge can't fall or sway
and I have no inner, hidden fear to cross
but I just can't get up and walk away
even though I have this sense of loss.

It is the crucifixion of the mind.
With thoughts I'm nailed onto a shape
of ideas that I should have left behind

but which in my apathy I can't escape.
I can only dangle here, to dream and wait
'till hell's upon me and it is too late.

The wall

I'm up against this wall again -
a wall that will not let me through,
an obstacle of nagging pain
that keeps me separate from you.
I am cemented in its bricks,
It's all there ever seems to me,
and by its dark, delusive tricks
condemns me to this misery.
Is this, at last, then the end?
that claims I can only go this far?
and that I only can pretend
my way through this inner bar?
lest it was placed here to destroy
and convert my pain to joy!

The outmoded

The old ideas that are restricting me
I faithfully believed would set me free.
I thought their counsels worthy and secure
and that their timeless insights would endure!
It seemed that their solutions would apply
to every problem until I would die.
They promised such stability and hope,
the means and ability with which to cope,
demanding only that I firmly stay
on their road which is the only way!

Yet I find through experience and pain
roads change their course time and again,
and that to think their way is firmly set
is to travel on the highway of regret.

I see in my ideas that time eroded
only their insanity and harshness survives
for each moment that I live becomes outmoded
when the present one arrives.

The shape of death

Death takes on a sweeter shape
when our fears are withdrawn,
posing as the great escape
into a new and better dawn.
When the world is seen through
it's an ego jungle meanly vying
in each action that we do
with the flesh self-glorifying.
Then only emptiness remains
without a purpose or goal
because the intent that sustains
is now withdrawn from the soul,
that found its own sweet flesh to be
the home of lust and anarchy.

Advice

I hate the bloody way you scoff!
"There are many people much worse off!
You can still see for you're not blind
and you can yet reason with your mind.
I see you walk and, yes, you hear
and that you're healthy is all too clear!"

But I say to you: "I see him not!
and what is worse than this lot?
I walk but I go nowhere
on this tightrope of despair.
No more do I hear how he
speaks with me so tenderly.
My very health makes me ill
when I can't sense his noble will.

So what's the use when all I see
are surfaces painted with misery?
and to be healthy has no goal
when I am more than dead of soul.

And this state that you call well
is just a synonym for hell."

Truth and lies

The important thing to know
is what isn't really so

since the lies we know as fact
keep our ignorance intact.

To know the truth is better still
because it liberates the will

but to live the truth is the best
for thereby all of life is blest.

The reprieve

(Upon coming out of a long, dark night.)

I've been on death row for so long
the world outside has been forgotten
but in the cell where I belong
something priceless has gone rotten.
The scepter of the day of execution
has tarnished me with its pollution.

Then suddenly comes a new reprieve:
I am lead outside my lonely cell
and as I'm set free I can't believe
that I have been released from hell
where my mind has been so conditioned
life and death no longer are partitioned.

I lick freedom's sweetness from my lips.
Each breath permeates my lungs with cheer
and I feel how happiness swells and strips
from my vision the prison's false veneer
but I still wonder if it's just a make-believe
that sadistic jailers delight in to conceive.

My enemy

To have water that I can't drink,
that is how I feel you play with me.
You are the force with which I think
but which you will not let me be.

I believe but faith is not enough
to break through my aching lack
as I realize that I miss the stuff
to win the battle in my attack.

I wage a bitter war that I can't win
as my own desires are fighting me,
for they are the root of my sin
that makes you seem the enemy.

Lost in a dream

The result is swift when I stumble
and strikes the moment that I fall.
The game is set up to keep me humble
'till I learn to give my all.

But I'm tired of strife and struggle,
the battling with so little a spoil
of the ways I self-torture and juggle
through years of affliction and toil.

Yet I recall when we were united,
when no grief or sorrow or any pain
or being scorned or humbled or slighted
could force on my love any strain.

Even if the pain's not of my making,
or so unfair the load that I carry,
and my back feels that it is breaking,
it is worth the short moments You tarry.

For then all else is forgotten
and sorrow not what it may seem,
only a time that was misbegotten
when I was lost in a dream.

Names and forms

When I gaze at life through my mind
I see it fractioned into limitation,
but looking through trust in you I find
that forms transcend such obscuration
to be merely patterns that exist
in the belief of the self-hypnotist.

As I transcend their isness in the present
to become aware of your underlying hereness,
I find names and forms incandescent,
revealing to us your constant nearness,
so that we can penetrate and rise above
their boundries to your perfect love.

All objects pressure us to live in time
in which we always act as their effect,
but when we escape their pantomime,
that so enchants the intellect,
we discover that they celebrate
the joy you feel as you create.

Night life

A baby wakes up in the night
and searches for a glimpse of light
since the shadows that he sees
take on the forms of enemies.
That which makes his misery
can also help to set him free,
but no one teaches him the way
to break the mold of shadow clay.
And while he lays there in the cot,
bewailing his self-created lot
his cry becomes the very thing
that intensifies his suffering
for the dark that he perceives
takes on the form that he believes.

Unhooked thought

Suddenly my rigid soul was free
from ideas that held me in their chain
and I knew that my own mind's debris
caused the very fabric of my pain.
Every thought contributed a shade
from which my suffering was made.

It seems my mind's created to obey
thoughts upon which the will decides
and once made up there is no other way,
no new decision then overrides
'till the seed which was taken and sown
sprouted and grew in a wasteland zone.

Thus I must watch the mind's process
and realize that all thoughts impel,
and that they can doom and even bless
as they make for me a heaven or a hell
for as long as I give my mind free reign
I'll be its slave over and over again.

My belief is what I chose to accept
and act upon to give me happiness,
but because of them I have groaned and wept
lost in my stark and arid wilderness
where the thoughts I chose to set me free
enforced on me their bitter tyranny.

Now I am unhooked and thus will stay
as long as I remember to introspect,
to make sure that I know and then obey
the laws that are set up to protect
and bring all freedom to the soul
that willingly takes up this role.

A prelude to pain

Is this joy a prelude to new pain?
Must I go through more agony again?
to purify this contaminated heart
so you can fill it from end to start?

When I feel you this close to me
everything is so complete and free
that grief exists as a distant dream
which dried up like a desert stream.

But will new torrents come once more
to rush over the flowers on my shore?
dragging me along to unknown states
where life rots in death or stagnates?

For I have found that when I rejoice in you,
delighting in the rapture of your bliss,
it's to strengthen and prepare my mind anew
when pain creeps on like a slow paralysis.

Yet as I experience your presence, Lord,
the pain I suffered or bitterly resented,
is a small payment for the great reward
when my understanding is augmented.

Therefore I say in trembling and in fear:
Do with me what will cleanse and purify,
for when we're one it is all too clear
it is the shadow self that must die.

Behind closed eyelids

I close my eyes to find your solitude,
wrapped in a luscious warm and quiet;
beyond all noise and motion's feud
as thoughts and feelings stop their riot.
Though the world still roars and rushes,
this sanctuary keeps me sequestered,
away from which repels and crushes,
in which all my delusions festered.
Behind the doors of my closed senses
just you and I rejoice and dance,
and shamelessly all my pretenses
are slain in this divine romance
where what you are entices so
there's nowhere else I care to go.

When I don't love you

I dread the times not loving you . . .
When I am dry and feeling's fled,
and there is nothing I can do
to spur or raise the inner dead.

Then I exist without a care,
being, doing, having . . . all depressing,
and with you absent everywhere
I'm certain that I am regressing.

I seem not to love you anymore.
I've slid back into unconcern
for I have no urge to adore
the way my heart used to burn.

And even though I know right now
this state to be a passing phase
when I'm in it I feel somehow
I'll never exit from this maze.

I think I learn

I think I learn, but really don't.
My way is tortuous and hard,
for when I will I truly won't
since all my actions just retard
the progress that I yearn to make
but I'm destined to forsake.

It seems my ideas keep me blind
with thoughts repugnant to my nature
and they constantly mastermind
a self-imposed inner legislature
by creating conflicts that mislead
my feelings into death's stampede.

I can only look on with dismay
as my resolutions disintegrate,
and even as I protest and pray
my heart and mind will deviate
because what I am is contrary
to all that I am taught to be.

My limitless delight

You are my limitless delight,
the very love in which I dwell.
When I plug into your might
you make a heaven from each hell.

The very joy that I now feel
is you yourself disguised as me
that you express as you heal
me from delusions's tyranny.

O God, for whom I yearn and crave,
let this be my earthly song:
You are the ocean and I the wave
to whom your very depths belong.

Time and desire

You are contacted in the now -
absent in the future and the past.
It's in the present that you endow
the heart to move into the vast
where it finds your presence is
woven in its fabric as your bliss.

In the silent mind you are reflected
when thoughts and feelings have become still
and this vision becomes perfected
by the love with which you fill
everything that reveals how you
are ever present in the acts I do.

Retreating from the world's allure
I find you in all the things I see
where in the silence you endure
my endless self-made misery
until the day you give the boon
that I break out of my cocoon.

You let me go

You let me go! You let me go!
Oh, God, I wish it were not so,
for now that I don't really care
I do not see you anywhere!

My drive is cold. My joy is gone
and my heart will not go on,
making the effort to adore
when it can't love you anymore!
for since I have loved and lost
the effort seems not worth the cost.

Seagulls in the fog

Over London town the fog hangs many a day
as the peasoup blots the city lights away.
The streets are bleak like times of war and raid
only seagulls haunt the sky and cry afraid.

When the fog rolls in you hear their startled cry
as they wing the air where they are doomed to fly,
seeking for a place where they can settle down
while they circle over the hollow sounding town.

> Round and round and round they fly.
> Round and round and round they mill,
> seeking in the chilly sky
> for a place that's warm and still.

One time I walked the river in a dream
where barges cut the silence like a scream.
My lonely heart was aching for new love
and was beating like the seagull wings above.

Footsteps echoed in the darkened day
but they always seemed to go the other way
and romance was nowhere for me to find
as my thoughts milled like seagulls in my mind . . .

A crash and then a gull fell to my feet
as it flew into a bridge that spanned the street.
I picked it up and knew that it was dead
and the wet I felt was lonely seagull red.

I stood there in the dark and how I cried
for it seemed as though my very soul had died.
Like a seagull in the fog I was in flight
searching for a warm and radiant light.

Round and round and round I fly.
Round and round and round I mill.
Seeking in the chilly sky
for a place that's warm and still.

But love's elusive and so hard to find,
forcing my thoughts like seagulls in my mind
to fly where there is not a friendly home
thus dooming me to endless search and roam.

Tell me

What is it that you want from me?
Tell me! Don't leave me to guess.
I can only wait in tired misery
to escape from this bleak distress.

Why do I see only walls for tomorrow?
while today is lusterless and dead.
I walk in the graveyard of my sorrow
seeing nothing but the same ahead.

My trust is all enwrapped in fear.
Where am I going? I can't see the way!
My own beliefs are so unclear
it seems they're designed to betray.

Yet I must dauntlessly step out and hope
that your hand is there to guide me,
so I can persevere to grope
when my own stress overrides me.

The escape from duality

How do I escape duality?
I asked the big ear of the night.
And how do I gain the one reality
when opposites confuse my sight?

Inside me I find love and hate,
pleasure and pain, right and wrong.
How can I crush them and relate
to the state where I belong?

As I kept searching in my mind
during the calm of meditation
it took me by surprise to find:
attachment caused all oscillation.

While I cling I'm the effect
of the one thing that I desire
which causes me then to neglect
the All to which I should aspire.

But when I master wrong with right
I can then let go of both.
Duality then loses might
and even speeds my inner growth.

Then detachment brings me liberation
from the pairs that shape my prison
and destroys the deviation
from which duality has risen.

The resurrection

When your sweetness permeates me
and my heart glows within my chest,
and your love inebriates me
then truly, truly am I blessed.

In this state there is no separation,
nothing beside the happiness I feel.
There also is no sensual sensation
that can destroy my tender heel.

What fear or pain or grief have I?
What is left for me to desire?
The one opponent that can crucify
is temptation's cleansing fire.

And when it strikes I'll have no fear
for I must just remember this:
that which I am when you are here
is nothing other than your bliss.

Then it matters not if I have realization,
or the liberation I was taught to crave,
for in this state of perfect contemplation
I too have risen from the grave.

Saving limitations

You came into my darkest night
to make it deep and darker still,
blinding my dulled and outer sight
with my own perverted will
until I'm forced to look inside
where my day and night have died.

You bind my acts with apathy
and curb my thoughts with limitation,
framing my moods with ennui,
sacking my dreams with desolation
because I believe in what I see
rather than on what you ask of me.

You keep me in this inner jail
that I constructed with my projection
and which I love and do not fail
to give its being my protection
because I keep my mind on each thing
rather on that from which they spring.

By doing this I see that I
must keep my vision fixed on you,
that even if I have to die
in this new light that I pursue
I will see that what I see
is meant to bring you out of me.

Contradictions

I seek you in a heart that's vast!
made of elements that often contradict,
for our human concepts can never last
when theories and thoughts restrict.

Sometimes I just need to adore,
and surrender to a loving power,
aching to feel the Self much more
when it starts to bud and flower.

At other times I feel so austere
my mind travels in high abodes
when I can't sense a there or here
nor that there are any signs or roads
save 'you and I' and 'I, one with you'
that make all my viewpoints equally true.

The great unknown

The city glitters like a lake of fire flies,
a mirage that shimmers far off in the cold.
Above the stars are strewn across the skies
as their nightly wanderings unfold.

I sit outside, reaching for the All alone,
aware that in the skies and earth
it's hidden from our eyes and All Unknown
but which gives all things their worth.

I sense it centers in my quiet chest
for here I feel a hunger and a yearning
that sets my restless heart a-burning
and opens me 'till I am fully possessed
when I realize that being has no limitation
and to assign one is to deepen my isolation.

Without goals

Without goals the mind gets lazy.
There is no room from which to expand
and our thoughts become feeble and hazy
because we cannot come to understand
that lesser ambitions create the space
where we can establish our own place.

Without desire the will is petrified
for want generates energy and aim.
The more the need the more it's amplified
until the heart sets out to claim
the universe which it must transcend
before it can reach the Endless End.

These interim desires must be strong
enough to keep mind on its track
so that it can feel and still belong
to the world, its real draw-back,
but weak enough to be disregarded
when at last they all must be discarded.

Though the traffic roars

Though the traffic roars and rushes
and people laugh and talk and scream,
and tension tightens as it crushes
inside I'm silent like a dream.

You're back and now I drift along
like a berg of ice within the sea,
lazing in the quiet song
of infinite, a symphony.

Since ice and water are the same
the I am that I am is you.
The only difference is the name
and form that we care to imbue.

We're one and in this thought I dwell.
Nothing can harm me in this state.
Here thoughts can never come and tell
the lies that cleave and separate.

Storm interlude

Night of wind and rain!
O God, how warm the cold
as it beats the window pane
like a lover over bold.

Just a memory of wind
rushing madly in the night
like a child undisciplined
sets my fantasy to flight.

And suddenly you are here,
and there and everywhere, and I?
All oscillations disappear
as we clash and unify!

I am the night, the wind and rain,
the person listening in the storm,
whose being lives just to attain
the formless that sustains my form!

The choice

The choice is very hard to make.
It seems I only want my will.
The trouble is I won't forsake
the very thing that makes me ill.

To face the dragon, that I must.
To slay the beast is my ambition
for in your power I can trust
to overcome my own sedition.

But all I do's exaggerate
by seeing a snake for the rope,
so I can then navigate
among the ways I need to cope.

I now begin to understand
the very first move must be mine
since by your will I'll always land
in the outstretched arms divine.

Desire bound

I bind myself with my own desires
and remain a prisoner of false delight.
My chains are forged in decision's fires
that I endow with a special might
to keep me writhing in the dirt
where I wallow in my secret hurt
and suck on them as though they're pacifiers.

I give up my peace to fight a war,
not against outside enemies and foes,
but my own tendencies that I adore
and that cause my endless woes.
Yet I see that my very sin
is just lack of self-discipline
that wanting endless forms never outgrows.

The evil that I think I am is just a graft,
a dream that someone else instilled in me,
who cast a spell with their witchcraft
and blossoms by what they willed in me,
but when I break attachment to their presence
and find you as my fundamental essence
then you destroy what was instilled in me.

Then why do I love the chains so much
that I will not wrench them from my wrists?
Because they have a comforting touch
and a reassurance that persists?
No, I see now its karma's friend delusion
that keeps me trapped in its illusion
by giving me a role my inner saint resists.

Just a little effort

Just a little effort and hope arises.
A new energy gushes forth that brings
desire and its myriad of surprises
to wipe out my needless sufferings.

I see my carelessness is self-instigated
with apathy as its maiden name,
and all its brood of sloth it generated
brought me humbled in my shame.

But I shall rise again and thus return
to my Father and as a servant I will toil
because I know that I can never earn
my freedom from the life I spoil.

Just to be near Him's more fulfilling
than what the intellect conceives
and for the heart that's ever willing
faith becomes what it believes.

Surrender

Place me where you need me, Lord.
Your will be done in every way.
All good and bad is underscored
with your presence come what may.

It does not matter how I feel,
what I do or where I go,
or if you decide not to heal
me from the foolishness I know.

Do with me what you chose,
or nothing if it be your will.
Let me know my way or lose
all whether I am well or ill.

Even if you would confuse me
I will love you all the same,
and if you decide not to use me
I'll still extol your holy name.

Demon dreams

Groping deeper and what do I find?
Anguished spaces that stretch nightwards,
where there is dissolution of the mind
and the soul inclines frightwards,
not wanting to pass through the state
that it can never contemplate.

Facing dreams so real they castigate,
and punish as though they control
every part of the life that I navigate
behind the masks of their deceiving role
since I think the truth can damage so
that it seems better for me not to know.

Yet one day I must cross this stream
and face my inner dragon on the way;
to slay for once the demon dream
that keeps my mind going astray
so I can find that which I feared
were only my own fantasies I reared.

With my feelingness

With my feelingness I see
the universe inside of me,
where dark is stipped of the night
and day's denuded of the light,
for the texture of my presence
expands endlessly its essence
to enlarge my fettered beingness
and secure my subtle seeingness
that beholds by being what it sees
and so dissolves all mysteries
until there is only I
that only I can occupy.

I'd like to shout

I'd like to shout from rooftops and towers
of the things you have recently done;
of the subtle way your power devours
my delusions and pains one by one.

How I was once a downtrodden slave
to my senses and what I was taught,
when I used to seethe and misbehave
when all my plans came to naught.

I'd like to shout how you freed me from fear
and the death I couldn't help living;
and how you helped me to persevere
in my surrender and acts of forgiving.

But most I'd tell how you dwell inside
and make my own world warm and sane
and that this heart in which you abide
has now become heaven again.

Index

151	Advice	145	Dream is the web
110	A gift of love	23	Dream learning
140	A hollow tube	43	Drugged by dreams
37	Always the same	16	Dual role
62	Amapola		
112	A moment of glory	29	Empty dreams
50	An only son	86	Eternal Spring
95	An overflow of love	100	Even when I don't love you
156	A prelude of pain	99	Everything reminds me of you
85	Assimilation	33	Evil is manifest in sin
50	A song of freedom		
67	A time bomb	82	Faith
119	A veiled romance	139	Finding you
89	A veil of lies	107	Fire child
118	A worn out role	137	Fooled by surfaces
		24	Four insights
157	Behind closed eyelids	32	Four new insights
32	Behind my thoughts	36	Free choice or not
123	Behind the emptiness I feel		
128	Between extremes	70	Groping
55	Born outside		
15	Breakthrough	69	Hallucinations
24	But when you leave	49	He is I
		96	Hidden music
38	Christ time	88	How glad I am
41	Come to me	105	How many dreams?
67	Confusion	113	How vast you are!
167	Contradictions	76	Hybernation
25	Could I but realize		
122	Crossroads	81	I am spring
136	Curtain time	24	I can't predict
		173	I'd like to shout
58	Dance eternal	129	If only . . .
77	Deeply content	44	I have stopped reaching
115	Desert silence	71	I know the truth
172	Demon dreams	40	I lie around
170	Desire bound	139	I listen for you to speak
82	Detachment	119	I live by faith
142	Dream counsel	162	I lost you
127	Dream identity	116	I love once more

19	Imprint	162	Out of the shadows
137	Imprisoned		
138	In the rain last night	135	Pain, the uninvited
48	In the silence	91	Plugged into you
27	Intruder		
61	In you I live	35	Running free
57	I recognize you		
34	Is it you, Lord?	166	Saving limitations
52	I sought for meaning	160	Seagulls in the fog
112	I sought you	109	Self-deception
158	I think I learn	163	Silence tells me
14	It shocks me	32	Since we are one
11	I walk a razor's edge	66	Slay this little self
103	I want to not want	144	Software
		98	Solitude
129	Jolt	124	Stages
171	Just a little effort	169	Storm interlude
53	Just let me rest	30	String bound
46	Just to be	171	Surrender
133	Let me die	161	Tell me
36	Liberty	113	The body
153	Lost in a dream	149	The bridge
10	Love and lust	109	The Buddha told me
		106	The catcher in the dream
26	Ma Durga	102	The chase
87	Misspent	169	The choice
152	My enemy	72	The closed door
9	My friend poetry	21	The daisy
74	My friends	97	The dance of creation
136	My insanity	17	The dancing warrior
158	My limitless delight	12	The divine conquest
39	My only sin	54	The door
130	My peace has come	73	The end has come
		164	The escape from duality
154	Names and forms	63	The face
114	New laughter	134	The failed system
154	Night life	120	The fall
148	No more	85	The freedom of eagles
42	No more self-lynching	65	The gap between us
51	No objection	28	The geranium
30	Not knowing	28	The glow of sin
		16	The great dawning
140	Obedience	167	The great unknown
74	Only you as I	132	The grinding
143	Out of nothing		

175

75	The grin of death	155	Unhooked thoughts
13	The hummingbird	104	Unyoking
27	The imposter		
79	The jail	45	Veiled in pain
126	The kiss divine	61	Victim soul
127	The leash of my senses		
101	The letter of the law	52	Wearied
131	The Master	110	We buy into lies
31	The movie show	94	What I am
64	The no-place	83	What Jesus taught
56	The omnipresent heart	14	When everyone is sleeping
150	The outmoded	84	When he comes
81	The owl	65	When hell is over
90	The pain	157	When I don't love you
128	The pot of gold	29	When I drift
80	The power of the vow	123	When I plan
141	The prodigal	142	When I read your words
26	The rainbow's end	95	When I run away
152	The reprieve	147	When my heart and mind run dry
165	The resurrection	93	When you are all I want
141	The right decision	25	When your bliss delights
22	The runaway	146	Whom you are
108	The senses	46	Who you are
150	The shape of death	99	Why should I want to see you?
60	The smile of God	47	Winter's price
96	The stillness binds	126	Within my heart
118	The stone	69	Within your silence
68	The stripping	172	With my feelingness
48	The surprise	168	Without goals
69	The turtle dove	134	Without relevance
34	The unexpected	20	Wondering what freedom is
71	The waiting		
149	The wall	78	You are my omnipotence
59	The wall of dreams	116	You are the love I feel
10	The world I see	114	You can be met with
115	The world of silence	125	You come as dusk
7	Thou art the singer	111	You come to me
168	Though the traffic roars	159	You let me go
159	Time and desire	100	Your commandments enebriate
86	To forgive	31	Your holiness
92	Total satisfaction	33	Your native state
151	Truth and lies	18	You wake so gently
		121	You welcome me
102	Under attack	80	Your will
117	Understanding		

Current Books from Wenzel Press

THE BIBLE MAY AGREE WITH EVOLUTION, AND SCIENCE MAY AGREE WITH THE FLOOD. 122 illustrations including 23 full-page B&W photos. Offers proof that the Bible never disagrees with evolution. Doesn't conflict with Pope Pius' encyclical on evolution. Offers 10 chapters of possible proof for the world-wide flood, and includes scientific proof that God exists.

RUNNING FREE. 237 poems by Sebastian Temple, world-famous composer of the *Prayer of St. Francis* and other Catholic songs. His first book of rhythmic, rhyming poems is powerful, thought-provoking and deeply prayerful. Many of the poems end with surprising insights.

ST. TERESA'S CASTLE OF THE SOUL: A STUDY OF THE INTERIOR CASTLE. Explains St. Teresa's teachings on prayer by taking a few chapters at a time of the *Interior Castle*, but also comparing it constantly with all her other writings. Includes analysis of her writing style, the times she lived in, and adds three doctrinal studies of her visions.

ST. JOHN OF THE CROSS AND THE DARK NIGHT: *Understanding His Ascent and Dark Night in Easy Stages.* Explains St. John's books on prayer, taking a few chapters at a time. Completes St. John's outlines when St. John doesn't complete them himself. Includes 11 full-page B&W photos of peaceful mountain scenes to add to the meditative mood.

ASCENT OF THE MOUNT: THE LIFE AND WORKS OF ST. JOHN OF THE CROSS, 90-minute color video. Describes St. John's dramatic 16th-century life with hundreds of scenes depicting his life. Quotes his beautiful poetry which uses nature scenes to describe prayer, with 40 strikingly beautiful nature scenes to illustrate them. Video praised world wide.

HOMILIES FOR LIVING THE FAITH. Challenging homilies by a Carmelite hermit priest, covering the three-year cycle of Sundays. Always discusses the appropriate Scripture passages and includes little-known facts and history, inspiring the reader/listener to consult the Scriptures. Never uses personal experiences or condemns the past to push something new.